SECOND EDITION

# TAKE YOUR TRICKS

OVER 550 DECLARER PLAY TIPS
YOU CAN TAKE TO THE BANK

EDWIN B. KANTAR

SECOND EDITION

# TAKE YOUR TRICKS

OVER 550 DECLARER PLAY TIPS
YOU CAN TAKE TO THE BANK

ISBN 13: 978-1-58776-164-5

Library of Congress Number:
2008923111

Bridge Book
Manufactured in the United States of America

675 Dutchess Turnpike, Poughkeepsie, NY 12603
www.vivisphere.com (800) 724-1100

# TABLE OF CONTENTS

# PUBLISHER'S NOTE

Eddie Kantar has long been renowned for the ease with which he is able to impart great gobs of information, the reader smiling all the while. Nowhere is that more evident than in his three "Tips" books.

"Take Your Tricks" is a compendium of critically useful information on the play of the hand. Condensed into easily digestible bits, and flavored with the well-known Kantar humor, this book can be used as a reference for eons to come. And if you should wear out your copy through constant use, not to fret. This printing will always be available, thanks to the advantages of on-demand technology.

Watch for the similarly effective "tips" books on bidding and defensive play.

*Ron Garber*
*for SQueeZe Books*

# INTRODUCTION

I have written another book of tips, this one on the play of the hand. The book is aimed at almost any player beneath "expert" level who genuinely wishes to improve his or her game a notch or three.

Unlike the bidding tips book, these tips are not controversial. You can take them to the bank. With over 550 tips coming at you, you can be sure some of them have appeared in print before. Most have not. As I was writing this book I saw a common thread emerging. If you seriously wish to improve your play of the hand you must:

1. Learn to look at the hand as an entire unit, trying not to focus on just one suit;

2. Form some battle plan;

3. Pay attention to their bids and PASSES;

4. Watch their leads and signals;

5. Give sensible opponents credit for having some reason behind their plays;

6. Know how to force defensive errors;

7. Count everything in sight, their points, their distribution, and their tricks. And don't forget to count YOUR tricks!

If you already do all of these things, there is no need to buy a copy of this book. Instead buy one for your partner who must be lacking in some of these categories—otherwise why aren't you winning everything?

Another hidden plus; after your partner reads this book and starts making more contracts, you will think that your bidding has improved. With the exception of the last chapter entitled "Matchpoint Tips," the book is aimed at teaching you how to make your contract. Risking the contract for overtricks is not a consideration.

I must thank all my proofreaders though one accused me of being a commaholic. In spite of all of the wonderful corrections that were made, I perversely made more changes. Therefore, all remaining errors are mine.

In dealing with the dreaded "he"/"she" problem I decided to use "he" for simplicity. If this offends any woman reading the book, I apologize. The title of this book was also a problem. The two that hurt the most to dismiss were:

1. Bridge, Sex, Violence, Part I Bridge;

2. The Mother of All Tip Books.

Finally, if anyone had written a book like this when I was an emerging player, it would have saved me years of effort—he added modestly.

Eddie Kantar

# CHAPTER 1

# WARM UP TIPS

1. Review the bidding, including original passes.

2. Remember the opening lead. (Repeat it to yourself). Low spot card leads are particularly easy to forget.

3. Consider how long the opening leader took to make the opening lead. Did it whistle out there or was there a little suffering? This could be important later when trying to construct a picture of the opening leader's hand.

4. Know your opponents' lead and signaling conventions BEFORE play begins. It is better not to have to ask revealing questions later.

5. Ask yourself what the opponents know about YOUR strength and distribution from the bidding. Say your bidding has shown 7-10 HCP and as the play progresses, you have turned up with 8 HCP. They know you have no more aces or kings.

6. After any lead they make, ask yourself how much the opponents know about your holding in that suit. Do they know your length? Do they know which honors (or spot cards) you hold? If so, try to play those cards as quickly as possible, perhaps sooner.

7. Do not let the opponents know by any mannerism or comment how you feel about your contract. It gives away too much information.

8. Do not get into the habit of pulling a card out, putting it back, etc. Make up your mind which card you are going to play and then play it.

9. Do not put short suits on either end of your hand. Put them in the middle. Some players notice where cards come from.

10. Hold your cards back when you play, way back. A word to the wise.

11. If a suit or a number of suits break badly for you, take it in stride. Moaning and groaning is for professional wrestlers.

12. Do not play from trick to trick. Formulate some plan, any plan!

13. The quickest road to disaster is to stop thinking about the contract you are in—thinking instead about the contract you wish you were in. Before you know it, you will be playing the hand as if you were in that other contract.

14. Don't destroy the partnership by getting on your partner after he has misplayed a hand. Save discussions for after the game. Keep the criticism constructive, not destructive.

15. If you happen to win a trick with an unexpectedly low card, conceal your glee until the end of the hand. If you let on what has happened (one opponent will know anyway), it can't help your side. The most likely scenarios are that (1) someone has a pulled a wrong card; (2) someone has a hidden card; (3) the opening leader has underled his life looking for a ruff; (4) you are playing against a blood relative.

16. After you lead to a trick wait for second hand to play. Do not call for a card (tournament play) or reach to take a card from dummy (rubber bridge) before second hand plays. If you do, fourth hand is allowed to play out of turn. This, in turn, gives second hand a chance to see partner's card before playing to the trick.

17. Assume your partner is playing the hand and a spade is led. When you put your dummy down, put down your spades LAST. This forces your partner to look over your beautiful dummy before, perhaps, playing too quickly to the first trick.

18. Assume you are dummy in a notrump contract. During the bidding both you and partner have bid hearts. When the lead is made, do not put your hearts down on your extreme right. Partners have been known to lose it and play the hand as if hearts were trumps!

19. Do not snap your cards when playing to a trick.

20. When dummy comes down, add your high card points to dummy's high card points. This will tell you how many high card points the opponents have. If they have been in the bidding this count might be quite helpful. Assume you become declarer after your LHO has opened 1NT (16-18). You discover that you have 23 HCP between your hand and dummy.

Conclusion: RHO can have no more than a jack!

# CHAPTER 2

# READING THE OPENING LEAD AT SUIT CONTRACTS

The opening lead helps build a picture of the opponents' hand. If you pay careful attention to the card that has been led plus third hand's play to the trick, you should have a good idea of what is going on in at least one of the suits. In addition, certain inferences can be drawn from what was NOT led.

21.  If you are missing the ace in the suit that has been led, assume your RHO has the ace and play accordingly.

22.  If the opponents do not lead a suit in which you are missing both the ace and the king, assume the honors are split or RHO holds them both.

23.  If you are missing both the king and the queen of an unbid suit and that suit is not led, assume the honors are split or RHO has them both.

24.  If you are missing the AKQ of a suit that has been bid to your left and not led, assume the AQ is to your left and the king to your right.

25.  If a short suit is led, assume trumps are breaking evenly. Players with four trump seldom lead from short suits.

26.  If your trump suit is weak and your final game contract has not been doubled, assume a civilized trump division.

27.  If the bidding has indicated that dummy has a likely long suit and a trump is led, assume the long suit is NOT dividing evenly.

28.  If you have bid two suits and wind up in your second suit, a trump lead usually indicates that the opening leader has strength in your first suit.

29.  Strong players are more apt to lead from kings than from jacks. However if your bidding has shown a powerful balanced hand, do not assume the opening lead is from a king.

30.  When RHO bids a suit and LHO leads a trump, LHO has: (1) a balanced hand with honors in each suit; (2) Axx in partner's suit and fears you may have the king; (3) a hearing disorder.

31.  A player who leads a short suit instead of the suit that has been bid and supported either has trump control or is desperate.

32.  A player who leads a short suit seldom has the queen of trumps. Play RHO for the queen.

33.  Most defenders lead a singleton if they have one. However a strong defender will NOT lead a singleton: (1) vs. a voluntarily bid slam holding an outside ace; (2) in a side suit you have bid strongly; (3) holding a natural trump trick(s) (QJx, J10xx, etc.).

34.  When a player bids a suit strongly and then leads a strange looking card in the suit, he is probably under leading his life holding a side suit void. If dummy has something like 10xx, Jxx or Qxx facing a singleton in your hand, consider playing high from dummy and don't faint if dummy's card wins the trick.

35.  Some players tend to make aggressive leads; others lean toward passive leads. The more you know about your opponents' leading tendencies, the easier it is to work out what the lead is from.

36.  When the unbid suit is not led, the two most likely reasons are: (1) the opening leader has the ace of the suit; (2) the opening leader has a strong lead in another suit.

37.  An ace is most likely to be underled when dummy has bid notrump and you have shown a very weak hand.

38.  A player who preempts usually has a singleton. If it isn't led, it is probably in the trump suit.

39.  It is important to know which card the opponents lead from three or four small. It is equally important to know which card they lead from an AK combination.

40.  If a jack or queen is led and you can see the honor directly beneath in either your hand or dummy, assume the opening leader has a singleton or a doubleton.

41.  If a ten is led and you can see the nine, assume the opening leader has either a singleton or a doubleton. However if the opponents are leading the ten from KJ10, you cannot make this assumption.

4

# CHAPTER 3

# LEADS VS. NOTRUMP

42. If LHO leads a short suit, chances are his long suit(s) has been bid by either you or dummy.

43. If the opening lead is in a suit that you have bid, or perhaps rebid, chances are the opening leader has five reasonable cards in that suit. Holding fewer it is unlikely he would lead the suit.

44. If the lead turns out to be from a four card suit and the opening leader later turns up with a singleton, assume an original distribution of 4-4-4-1. Otherwise, the opening leader would have led from a five card suit.

45. Be familiar with your opponents' honor lead conventions.

46a. *The Jack:* If the jack denies a higher honor, you can immediately place all the missing honors to your right. If it does not, allow for KJ10 or AJ10.

46b. *The Ten:* If the ten is a standard lead, it will either be top of a sequence or from an interior sequence headed by the A109, K109 or Q109. If the ten shows zero or two higher, it will either be from the top of a sequence or from a KJ10 or an AJ10 combination. Look for the jack. If you can see it, assume top of a sequence. If you can't see it, assume the stronger holding.

    You can further double check by looking for the nine. If you can see it, assume the lead is from the KJ10 or the AJ10. If you can't see the nine and you can't see the jack, it isn't clear which holding the opening leader has—although it is more likely to be from one of the stronger holdings.

46c. *The Nine:* Some play that the nine is either top of a sequence or, more likely, from a combination headed by the A109, K109 or Q109. When a nine is led, look for the ten. If you can see it, the lead is top of a sequence, if you can't see it, assume the lead is from one of the stronger holdings.

47. When RHO overcalls and LHO leads another suit, the presumption is that the opening leader either has a singleton in partner's suit, a strong suit of his own or has seen his partner's overcalls before.

48. If LHO bids one suit and then leads another, assume a two-suiter.

49. The lead of a queen can be either the top of a sequence or from an AQJ combination. The sequence lead is far more likely.

50. Be aware of which card the opponents have agreed to lead from three small, four small or five small.

51. If an opponent takes a long time to make an opening lead, you can make several inferences: (a) the opening leader has a difficult hand to lead from; (b) if an honor card is finally led—say the queen, do not count on it being from a QJ10 combination.

# CHAPTER 4

# THE FIRST TRICK

It is no secret that many contracts are lost at the very first trick. There are oodles of reasons. (1) Playing too quickly. (2) Winning the trick in the wrong hand. (3) Playing the wrong card from dummy. (4) Playing the wrong card from your hand. In order to avoid some of these possible pitfalls, study these tips. The East-West cards may not be shown. In most of the diagram positions you will see only your hand and dummy.

Assume West leads a low card (x). If East's play is relevant, it will be shown. Otherwise it will be designated with a ?. Unless stated differently, the proper play at trick one is the same whether the contract is suit or notrump.

52. When ALL of the spot cards in your hand are equal to that of an honor in dummy, for deceptive purposes, play the honor from dummy.

|  | **North** (dummy) | |
|---|---|---|
|  | 103 | |
| **West** | | **East** |
| x | | J |
|  | **South** | |
|  | AK9 | |

Play the ten. If this is covered with the jack, West will not be able to place the nine. If you play low from dummy and East plays the jack, West will know that you have the nine.

53. Do not waste a spot card from dummy if you have an equal spot card in your hand along with a LOWER non-equal spot card.

|  | **North** (dummy) | |
|---|---|---|
|  | 103 | |
| **West** | | **East** |
| J7654 | | Q8 |
|  | **South** | |
|  | AK92 | |

West leads the five. Play LOW from dummy to ensure three tricks. If you squander the ten, you only get two tricks.

54.
                    **North** (dummy)
                    92
**West**                                      **East**
J7654                                    10
                    **South** (you)
                    AKQ83

West leads the five. Play LOW from dummy to ensure four tricks. If you squander the nine, you only get three. Note: If your holding was AKQ8, then you should play the nine in order to conceal the eight from LHO.

55.    The significance of the ten either in the dummy or in your own hand, should not be overlooked.

                    **North** (dummy)
                    1032
**West**                                        **East**
x                                         ?
                    **South** (you)
                    KQ5

Versus notrump, play the ten. This gains a trick when West has led from the ace and the jack.

56.
                    **North** (dummy)
                    A108
**West**                                        **East**
x                                         ?
                    **South** (you)
                    K43

Play the eight. If this drives out an honor, you can finesse the ten later.

57.
                    **North** (dummy)
                    A103
**West**                                        **East**
x                                       ?
                    **South** (you)
                    K65

Versus notrump, play the ten. West may have led from the QJ.

Versus suit, play low. West is unlikely to have both honors (would have led the queen) so you must hope that East, with one honor (likely), errs by playing that honor instead of a lower spot card.

58.

**North** (dummy)
K10

**West**
x

**East**
?

**South** (you)
Q43

Play the ten. If West has led from the jack, you are assured of two tricks.

59.

**North** (dummy)
K4

**West**
x

**East**
?

**South** (you)
Q107

Play low from dummy to ensure two tricks in the suit. Play the same if dummy has Qx and you have K10x or A10x.

60. Knowing that the opening leader will seldom underlead an ace at a suit contract opens up new avenues of thought.

**North** (dummy)
KQ10x

**West**
2

**East**

**South** (you)
x

The ace is marked with East and the lead of a low card generally shows an honor. If you need two side suit discards, insert the 10. Even if it loses to the jack (unlikely), later you can lead the king and take a ruffing finesse through East's known ace and get your trick back.

61. There are many times when it is almost mandatory to play high from dummy.

**North** (dummy)
K4

**West**
x

**East**
x

**South** (you)
Q7

Versus notrump, play the king. If the king holds, West may not be sure your queen is blank. With the king and queen reversed, play the queen from dummy for the same reason.

62.

                                **North** (dummy)
                                Q6

**West**                                              **East**
x                                               ?

                                **South** (you)
                                1043

Versus notrump, play the queen. Your only chance to score a trick is if West has underled the AK.

63.

                                **North** (dummy)
                                K4

**West**                                              **East**
x                                             ?

                                **South** (you)
                                J107

Versus notrump, play the king. If West has the ace and East the queen, they can easily have problems. Versus suit, play low. East is marked with the ace.

64.

                                **North** (dummy)
                                K4

**West**                                              **East**
x                                             ?

                                **South** (you)
                                J65

Versus notrump, play low to ensure one trick. However if you are WIDE OPEN in another suit, play the king to minimize the risk that East will win the trick. Versus suit, play low. The ace is marked with East.

65.    Good declarers envision possible blocked suits.

                                **North** (dummy)
                                A9

**West**                                              **East**
x                                             Jx, Qx or Kx
                                **South** (you)
                                10xxx

Versus notrump, play the ace. If the suit is divided 4-3, it won't matter what you do. However if the suit is divided 5-2 and East has a doubleton honor, the suit is blocked.

66. With 109xx in either hand facing Jx, Qx or Kx, one notrump trick is guaranteed if you play low from dummy.

**North** (dummy)
Jx, Qx or Kx

**West**
x

**East**
?

**South** (you)
109xx

Play low from dummy. If the North-South cards are reversed, also play low from dummy.

67. When RHO is known to have the AJ9x(x) hovering over the Q10x or K10x in dummy (you having Qxx or Kxx), playing high from dummy completely disrupts their communication.

**North** (dummy)
Q104

**West**
83

**East**
AJ975

**South** (you)
K62

East has bid the suit and West leads the eight. Play the queen from dummy. If East wins the ace, he cannot continue the suit without giving up a trick. If East ducks, you make a second trick with the king. The play of the queen cuts their lifeline.

68. If you can afford to play a meaningless honor card from dummy in order to coax third hand to cover, by all means play the honor.

**North** (dummy)
J104

**West**
x

**East**
?

**South** (you)
AK or AQ

Play the ten (or jack). If East has the missing honor, he may play it. It costs you nothing to try.

69. If it can cost you a possible trick to play an honor from dummy to coax an errant cover, do not play the honor from dummy.

**North** (dummy)
J1043

**West**
x

**East**
?

**South** (you)
AK or AQ

Given this layout, you have three tricks if you play low from dummy. If you play an honor and East plays low (East may not even have the missing honor), in all likelihood you will have squandered a trick.

70. When the dummy has J9 or Q9 doubleton, you should be familiar with these trick one plays.

**North** (dummy)
J9

**West**
x

**East**

**South** (you)
AQ2

For three tricks, play the nine. West may have the ten and East the king. Play the jack (instead of the nine) only if you are "sure" West has the king.

71.
**North** (dummy)
J9

**West**
x

**East**

**South** (you)
Axx

Play the jack. Your only chance for two tricks is if West has underled the KQ. With A10x also play the jack to conceal the ten. If East covers the jack, West will not know who has the ten. If you play the nine and East plays an honor, West will know.

72.
**North** (dummy)
Q9

**West**
x

**East**

**South** (you)
AJx

For three tricks, play the nine. East may have the king and West the ten. Play the queen (instead of the nine) if you are "sure" West has the king.

# CHAPTER 5

# PLANNING THE PLAY AT SUIT CONTRACTS

Try to form the habit of looking at the entire hand rather than just one suit. Form some sort of provisional plan and be ready to change that plan if unexpected developments arise. Start watching and counting early.

73. Count losers. The three main ways of avoiding losers are: (1) ruffing them in the short hand; (2) discarding them on a long suit; (3) forcing the opponents to lead a suit that will cost them a trick.

74. Count losers in the hand that has the longer trump holding. The long hand might be the dummy, possibly after a transfer sequence.

75. The long hand can become the short hand! If the trump suit is originally divided 5-4 and you trump twice in the hand that has five trump, the four card trump hand becomes the long hand. Count losers from the new long hand.

76. When counting losers, differentiate between immediate losers (losers that the opponents can take when they next get the lead) and eventual losers, i.e. losers in suits that you still control.

77. Bridge hands often fall into recognizable types: mirrored distribution, long side suit in dummy, shortness in dummy with no long side suit, shortness in dummy plus a long side suit, problems in one suit only and scrambling hands where none of the above exist Once you can recognize the general hand type, you have taken the first giant step.

78. Think throw-in or end play when you and dummy have mirrored distribution.

79. Long strong side suits can only be taken in peace if (1) the opponents have been depleted of trump; (2) you have a reentry to dummy in those cases where the opponents have a high trump at large.

80. Hands with shortness in the dummy and no side suit to establish lend themselves to ruffing losers in the dummy. Entries to the long hand are necessary.

81. Dummies with both a long suit and a short suit offer various possibilities. It is usually right to threaten the opponents by playing the long suit first—provided dummy has enough entries to make the threat viable.

82. If a hand boils down to the play of just one suit, determine exactly how many tricks you need in that suit and play accordingly. More on this in the section entitled "Card Combinations".

83. As a rule, treat equally divided suits that have slow losers (Axx facing Kxx) as you would a snake. These are suits the defenders, not you, should be attacking.

84. If you feel you are in a great contract, ask yourself what can possibly go wrong and then play to avoid that possibility (safety plays).

85. If you feel you are in a wildly optimistic contract (partner has overbid again), assume the cards are favorably placed and play on that assumption.

86. At any given moment you must know how many trump are outstanding. The subtraction technique works well. Assume you have a total of eight trump leaving the opponents five. Say you draw one round of trump, both following, leaving them THREE. This technique works particularly well when you are playing a seven card trump fit and one opponent or another trumps in early.

87. Don't be oblivious to their leads and signals. How many times have you wished you had paid a little more attention?

88. The opening lead usually gives you either count, honor information or both. Put it all in your memory bank.

89. Nine out of ten signals are either attitude or count signals. Opponents are supposed to tell you their tendencies in this regard. Ask.

90. A big part of your game plan is protecting unprotected honors (Kxx facing xx or xxx) from a premature attack through the honor.

91. Never underestimate the importance of a concealed five or six card suit in the closed hand. It frequently is worth one or two tricks in the play.

92. It is not always easy to determine whether an attitude signal or discard is encouraging or discouraging. Assume an opponent follows suit or discards an "attitude" (opposed to a count) four spot.

    Look for the two LOWER missing spot cards, the deuce and the three. If you can see them both, the four is discouraging. If you see neither, assume the four is encouraging. If you can see only one, it is not clear. Therefore a seven may be a discouraging signal (if you can see all of the lower spots) and a three may be an encouraging signal if the deuce is not visible. LOOK BENEATH.

93. With Axx(x) in your hand facing xx in dummy, it is usually right to duck the first lead and win the second. This also applies when dummy has Axx(x) and you have xx. The play cuts the opponents' lines of communication, particularly when one opponent has a doubleton.

94. Promotion of cards is important. If the first trick is comprised of three or four top honors, eventually sixes and sevens assume starring roles.

95. When the problem appears to be forging reentries to your hand, you can open lines of communication by leading a singleton early in the play.

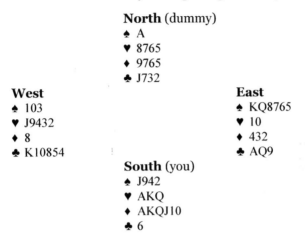

**North** (dummy)
♠ A
♥ 8765
♦ 9765
♣ J732

**West**
♠ 103
♥ J9432
♦ 8
♣ K10854

**East**
♠ KQ8765
♥ 10
♦ 432
♣ AQ9

**South** (you)
♠ J942
♥ AKQ
♦ AKQJ10
♣ 6

After East opens one spade, you wind up in six diamonds and West leads the ♠10. With a club loser staring you in the face, you must plan to ruff THREE spades in dummy. As it is risky to enter your hand more than once in hearts, begin by leading a club. Now you have the wherewithal to ruff three losing spades, returning to your hand only once in hearts. If you don't lead the club early, you put your slam at risk.

96. Don't fall victim to one of the most common of declarer maladies: ruffing losers in the dummy prematurely. When dummy has both a long suit with entries plus a short suit, begin by attacking the long suit.

**North** (dummy)
♠ K87654
♥ K54
♦ J
♣ Q92

**South** (you)
♠ 3
♥ Q107
♦ A97
♣ AK10843

Your contract is 5♣ and the lead is a low diamond to the king and ace. Begin by leading a spade. Let the play develop.

# CHAPTER 6

# NOTRUMP PLAY

Notrump play is actually easier than suit play. The main concern is TRICKS, setting up and taking your tricks before they can set up and take theirs. Think of notrump as a race where they get a headstart because of the lead. However you get to see partner's hand—the great equalizer.

97. Count your tricks and keep a RUNNING COUNT of your tricks as the play develops.

98. Be aware of the number of tricks the OPPONENTS can take at any given moment. Your battle plan is dependent upon this.

**North** (dummy)
♠ AJ8
♥ 10732
♦ Q1084
♣ 96

**West**
♠ 1043
♥ A95
♦ 72
♣ Q10843

**East**
♠ Q95
♥ K86
♦ J965
♣ KJ5

**South** (you)
♠ K762
♥ QJ4
♦ AK3
♣ A72

The contract is 1NT and West leads the ♣4. You win the third club discarding a heart from dummy. As the carding suggests that West has a five card suit, you stand to lose two more clubs plus two hearts the next time the opponents gain the lead. That comes to six tricks. On the plus side you have six tricks; two spades, three diamonds and a club. Who will get to seven first? You will if you knock out the ace-king of hearts, tricks YOU HAVE TO LOSE IN ANY EVENT. Do not set up their seventh trick by attacking either diamonds or spades.

99. It is almost always right to attack your longest suit to develop extra tricks. However if "time" is a factor, you may have to work with a shorter suit.

**North** (dummy)
♠ 3
♥ K9
♦ AQ109872
♣ Q83

**South** (you)
♠ AKQ42
♥ A8
♦ 65
♣ KJ104

You are playing 3NT and West leads the ♥Q. With six top tricks, you need to develop three more and QUICKLY. Attack clubs, not diamonds, for three sure tricks. Diamonds may produce more tricks, but you may have to let them in twice to get those tricks. You don't have time (enough heart stoppers) to let them in twice.

100. When "time" is NOT a factor, attack suits in which you are destined to lose tricks in any event: suits missing the ace, the ace-king, or even the ace-king-queen.

**North** (dummy)
♠ J103
♥ KQ72
♦ K43
♣ Q65

**South** (you)
♠ 9842
♥ A54
♦ AJ2
♣ AK4

Partner raises your 1NT opening to 3NT (no Stayman with 4-3-3-3 distribution) and the lead is the ♥3. You have eight tricks and should attack SPADES for your ninth-the suit where you have to lose tricks in any event.

101. Playing notrump contracts means dealing with the "danger" hand. The danger hand is either: (1) the opponent who has winners in a suit in which his partner is void; (2) the opponent who can lead through an unprotected honor. The idea is to keep the danger hand off play... at any cost!

102. Even strong looking suits must be handled with TLC in order to keep the danger hand off play.

**North** (dummy)
♠ 6
♥ K732
♦ AK10765
♣ A4

**South** (you)
♠ AJ7
♥ A84
♦ Q9
♣ QJ532

Versus your 3NT West leads the ♠5 to East's king. Looking over the entire hand you see that you have four sure tricks OUTSIDE of diamonds, your main suit, so you can afford to lose one diamond trick.

Because of the precariousness of your spade stopper, it is right to win the ♠A, cross to dummy with a heart and lead a low diamond to the NINE. This avoidance play protects you against East holding ♦Jxxx, the one combination that can harm you.

103. As an addendum to the previous tip, consider this card combination:

|  | **North** (dummy) KQ983 |  |
|---|---|---|
| **West** |  | **East** |
|  | **South** (you) A2 |  |

Assume you have outside dummy entries and you need only FOUR tricks from this suit. If WEST is the danger hand, play the ace and low to the nine. If EAST is the danger hand, run the nine. This play guards against the danger hand holding either 10xxx or Jxxx.

104. An even more common card combination lends itself to keeping the danger hand off lead:

|  | **North** (dummy) A765 |  |
|---|---|---|
| **West** |  | **East** |
|  | **South** (you) KJ1043 |  |

Say you need FOUR tricks and West is the danger hand. Lead the king and run the jack. If East is the danger hand, play the ace and then low to the jack.

105. Bottom line tip on the danger hand: To retain your health arrange for the danger hand to play second, not fourth, when taking a finesse.

106. Look for extra chances in the play before taking finesses in suits where no additional trick establishment is possible.

**North** (dummy)
- ♠ AQ54
- ♥ K43
- ♦ 654
- ♣ AK9

**South** (you)
- ♠ 6
- ♥ AQJ
- ♦ AKQJ10
- ♣ 8432

You arrive at 6NT and West leads the ♥10. With 11 top tricks you need to develop but one more. First lead a club to the nine. Later, test the clubs. If clubs are not 3-3, you may have to take the dreaded spade finesse. There are squeeze possibilities, but the bottom line is to attack clubs before spades.

107. Assuming fourth best leads, if the lowest missing card is led assume a four card suit. If the lowest missing card isn't led, keep an eagle eye out for the LOWER ones.

**North** (dummy)
74

**West**
K1053

**East**
QJ62

**South** (you)
A98

West leads the three, not the lowest card available, and East's jack wins. If East makes the normal return of the deuce (original fourth best) assume a 4-4 division.

108.

**North** (dummy)
984

**West**
Q10532

**East**
KJ6

**South** (you)
A7

West leads the three. Again the deuce is not visible. You duck East's king. When East returns the jack, indicative of two remaining cards, assume a 5-3 split even if West cunningly conceals the deuce.

109. When third hand unblocks at trick one assume a doubleton honor.

**North** (dummy)
765

**West**
Q1032

**East**
K9

**South** (you)
A84

West leads the queen and East plays the king. Assume a singleton or more likely a doubleton in the East hand. With Kxx the normal play is the middle spot card to encourage. Given this scenario, you usually do best to win the SECOND round of the suit. East will be void and you retain a low card for throw-in possibilities. It doesn't get much better than that.

110. The Rule of Eleven is always there for you when a fourth best lead hits the table.

**North** (dummy)
AJ82

**West**
K10765

**East**
9

**South** (you)
Q43

West leads the six, dummy plays low and East plays the nine which you win. By applying "the rule", subtracting the card led (the six) from eleven, you discover that there are FIVE cards higher than the six in the THREE REMAINING HANDS— North, East and South. You can see four of those five cards between your hand and dummy. Ergo, East started with only one card higher than the six—in this case, the nine. The next time you attack this suit, lead low to the EIGHT.

111. If the "rule" doesn't work, don't panic! The opening lead was not fourth best. Perhaps it was top of nothing or low from three. You must READJUST your thinking.

**North** (dummy)
AQ2

**West**
7

**East**
J!

**South** (you)
1093

West leads the seven. The "rule" tells you that East has no card higher than the seven. Hopefully you play low but East produces the jack! The rule has not lied. West has not led fourth best. West might have led top of nothing, second high from four small or low from K87.

112. When dummy has xx and you have AJx, you may have some heavy thinking to do when RHO puts up a high honor.

**North** (dummy)
74

**West**
Q10832

**East**
K95

**South** (you)
AJ6

West leads the three and East plays the king. Your play is dictated by which opponent is likely to get in next. If it is EAST, HOLD UP until the third round.

If it is WEST, WIN the trick as you retain a stopper with West on play. If you cannot be sure, don't call me, I'll call you.

113. With xx(x) in dummy and KJx in your hand, again you must make a battlefield decision when LHO leads low and RHO plays the queen.

**North** (dummy)
743

**West**
A10852

**East**
Q9

**South** (you)
KJ6

West leads the five and East plays the queen. If East is likely to be on lead next, play low. If West is more likely to get in next, play the king. The same reasoning applies when dummy has small cards and you have KQx. If LHO leads a low card and RHO plays the ten or jack, duck the trick if RHO is apt to get in next. Take the trick if LHO is due to get in next.

114. Holding the AKx(x) in your hand facing small cards in the dummy, win the first trick with the king rather than the ace.

**North** (dummy)
87

**West**
J9432

**East**
Q106

**South** (you)
AK5

West leads the three and East plays the queen. If you wish to conceal your strength, win the king. Winning the ace arouses suspicions. If that were your only stopper, why didn't you hold up?

115. There are times when it is wrong to hold up with the ace. You may have another suit that is as weak or weaker than the one that has been led.

**North** (dummy)
♠ 962
♥ A75
♦ QJ1065
♣ K3

**South** (you)
♠ A83
♥ 94
♦ K932
♣ AQ54

You end up in 3NT and West leads the ♠4 to East's queen. Take the trick! If the lead is honest, West has four spades and East three. If you win the ♠A immediately and drive out the ♦A, you make your contract. If you duck the opening lead and East shifts to a heart, what is to become of you?

116. When you have Ax in your hand facing a singleton or doubleton in the dummy, do NOT hold-up.

**North** (dummy)
54

**West**          **East**
Q10832          KJ97

**South** (you)
A6

West leads the three and East plays the king. Do not hold up. Win the ace. If West is first to regain the lead, how can West know who has the jack? He may play you for AJx(x) and be afraid to continue the suit.

117. Hold-up plays are used to exhaust one opponent. If you know one opponent has a singleton, take the ace at once. If you know one opponent has a doubleton, take the ace on the second round, etc.

**North** (dummy)
654

**West**          **East**
KQJ109          32

**South** (you)
A87

If the bidding has marked East with a doubleton, win the second round of the suit.

118. Do NOT make a hold-up play when you plan to finesse INTO the hand that has established winners in the suit that has been led. Save at least one exit card in the opponent's suit. More often than not, you can use your exit card eventually to force a favorable lead.

After you open one club, West overcalls one spade and you wind up in 3NT. West leads the ♠K You have eight top tricks and need a ninth from hearts. Unfortunately the bidding has marked West with at least five spades and almost certainly the ♥K.

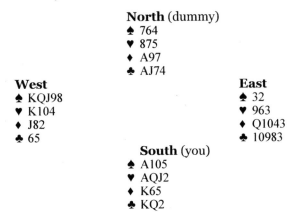

**North** (dummy)
♠ 764
♥ 875
♦ A97
♣ AJ74

**West**
♠ KQJ98
♥ K104
♦ J82
♣ 65

**East**
♠ 32
♥ 963
♦ Q1043
♣ 10983

**South** (you)
♠ A105
♥ AQJ2
♦ K65
♣ KQ2

Win the SECOND spade and rattle off four rounds of clubs. West has to make two discards. He is likely to discard a diamond and a heart. If he does, cash the ♦AK and exit a SPADE. West cashes his spade winners but in the end game must lead away from his ♥K into "jaws", your AQ. Had you won the third spade (primary school play), you would have to lead hearts first.

119.  With two stoppers in the suit that has been led, plus two aces to remove, hold up.

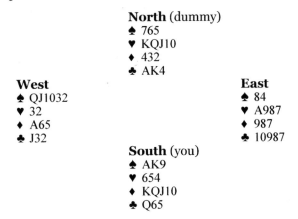

**North** (dummy)
♠ 765
♥ KQJ10
♦ 432
♣ AK4

**West**
♠ QJ1032
♥ 32
♦ A65
♣ J32

**East**
♠ 84
♥ A987
♦ 987
♣ 10987

**South** (you)
♠ AK9
♥ 654
♦ KQJ10
♣ Q65

West leads the ♠Q against your 3NT. You have to remove both red aces. Win the second spade voiding East. If the aces are split, you will not have to guess which ace to knock out first. When East gets in he will be spadeless. Had you won the first spade and attacked hearts, East would win and return a spade. When West gets in with the ♦A, curtains.

Give East three spades instead of two and you must knock out West's ace first. How are you supposed to know which ace West has? You're not; you have to be a good guesser.

120. With two stoppers and two cards to remove, you may be able to control which entry to remove first. Attack the entry, or the possible entry, of the player with the greater length in the suit that has been led.

**North** (dummy)
♠ 43
♥ 10654
♦ QJ105
♣ AK4

**West**
♠ QJ1098
♥ 87
♦ K87
♣ J32

**East**
♠ 652
♥ A932
♦ 64
♣ 10987

**South** (you)
♠ AK7
♥ KQJ
♦ A932
♣ Q65

You are playing 3NT and West leads the ♠Q. Win the second spade, cross to dummy with a club and finesse the diamond. After West has been defanged (his entry removed), knock out the ace of hearts. What if West has both entries? Why are you asking these terrible questions?

121. If you get lucky and the opponents do not lead your weakest suit, it might be right to take out a little insurance to protect against a later lead in the weak suit.

**North** (dummy)
♠ 852
♥ AQ52
♦ Q4
♣ AJ52

**West**
♠ A4
♥ J1098
♦ 1097
♣ Q87

**East**
♠ J9763
♥ 763
♦ KJ82
♣ 4

**South** (you)
♠ KQ10
♥ K4
♦ A53
♣ K10963

You are in 3NT and West leads the ♥J. You have avoided the diamond lead but there still could be be problems if West gets in early and leads a diamond. In order to make sure this does not happen, play the ♣K and a club to the jack. Even if the East wins the queen, you will have no further problem. You have time to set up your ninth trick in spades while your diamond position is intact.

122. Learn to appreciate the value of your lower cards. Do not treat them as orphans.

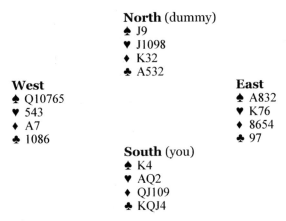

North (dummy)
♠ J9
♥ J1098
♦ K32
♣ A532

West
♠ Q10765
♥ 543
♦ A7
♣ 1086

East
♠ A832
♥ K76
♦ 8654
♣ 97

South (you)
♠ K4
♥ AQ2
♦ QJ109
♣ KQJ4

Once again you are playing the beloved 3NT and West leads the ♠6. East wins and returns the ♠2 to your king. With the setting tricks available in spades, you do not have "time" to drive out the ♦A. You must play on hearts.

Play the KQJ of clubs, overtaking the third round with the ace and run the ♥J. When that holds, continue with a heart to the queen and then the ace of hearts. You are now ready for your big moment. Lead the four of clubs to the five to take your ninth trick in hearts. Exchange the four and five of clubs between your hand and dummy and the hand cannot be made.

123. Of all the blunders, the worst is playing too fast to the first trick without counting your tricks.

North (dummy)
♠ AQJ
♥ 75
♦ K642
♣ J10864

South (you)
♠ 742
♥ A94
♦ QJ9
♣ AKQ3

25

Playing 3NT (what else?), West leads the ♠5. Plan your play. Looking at spades only, the correct play is the finesse. But looking at the hand as a unit you can ensure the contract by winning the ♠A and driving out the ♦A. If you finesse spades and it loses, a heart return is likely to defeat the contract. WHEN ONLY ONE LAYOUT OF THE CARDS CAN DEFEAT YOUR CONTRACT AND YOU CAN PROTECT AGAINST THAT LAYOUT, PROTECT!

# CHAPTER 7

# BIDDING AND PLAY INFERENCES

Once the dummy tables, inferences abound. When you can see how many cards you and your partner have in any suit or suits the opponents have bid, you may be able to work out how those cards are divided in their hands. In addition, you may be able to make similar inferences in an unbid suit. Making inferences in the play is also important. Most defenders have reasons for the plays they make. It is your job to figure out what they are. Additionally you must also work out what reasons they may have for NOT making certain plays.

## BIDDING INFERENCES

124. It is easier to make bidding inferences if you know THEIR system. Do they play 5 card majors? Which minor do they open with 4-4 in the minors? Do they open stronger minor with 3-3 in the minors or always one club? Do they tend to open light? Will they open 1NT with a 5 card major? Will they skip over a five or six card diamond suit to respond one heart or one spade to a one club opening? The more you know, the easier it is to defend.

125. When opener raises responder's suit and you see six cards in this suit between your hand and dummy, assume responder has four cards and opener three.

126. Assume LHO opens one diamond and RHO raises to two diamonds. When dummy tables, you see six diamonds between your two hands. Assume opener has three and responder four. These days nobody raises a minor directly with only three card support.

127. When a one club opener turns up with a three card club suit, play the opener for 4-4 in the majors or a 4-3-3-3 hand pattern with four cards in either hearts or spades, not diamonds.

128. If an opponent opens one diamond and turns up with a three card diamond suit, play the opener for 4-4 in the majors.

129. If both opponents have bid but neither has mentioned hearts, and you see a total of six hearts between your hand and dummy, assume hearts are divided 4-3. If either opponent had five hearts, the suit would have been mentioned. Your next job is to figure out who has four and who has three. Don't worry, you'll be able to do that in a year or two.

130. Same scenario only this time you can see only five hearts between your hand and dummy. Hearts figure to be 4-4. If either opponent had five, the suit would have been bid.

131. If the opponents have not bid and the dummy flops with xx in hearts facing xx, assume a 5-4 heart split.

132. Versus silent opponents, your dummy hits with a small singleton opposite a small doubleton heart. Assume a 5-5 adverse division. Presumably if somebody had a six card suit it would have been mentioned.

133. Versus silent opponents, your dummy hits and you see a total of two cards in a suit. You can make two assumptions: (1) the suit is divided 6-5, (2) one or both opponents has lost his voice.

134. The bottom line is that whenever the opponents have eight or more cards in an unbid MAJOR or 9 or more cards in any unbid suit, assume that the suit is divided as evenly as possible between their hands.

135. Assume LHO opens one spade, RHO bids 1NT and spades are never mentioned again. When your dummy comes down you see a total of six spades. Assume spades are 5-2. If opener had six, he would have rebid them.

136. When opener skips over a major suit either to rebid notrump or to rebid his original suit, assume he does not have four cards in that major. An exception would be those players who rebid 1NT with 4-3-3-3 distribution after a one level response (me, for example).

137. After a one spade response to a one club or a one diamond opening bid on what turns out to be a four card suit, assume responder does not have four hearts. With 4-4 in the majors, the likely response is one heart.

138. A player who makes a takeout double of one major usually has four cards in the other major, occasionally three—seldom fewer.

139. A player who doubles a minor suit opening bid normally has 4-4 or 4-3 in the majors.

140. Prepare yourself for off shape nonvulnerable preempts in third seat. Three bids with six baggers, weak twos on five card suits, etc.

141. Many partnerships use "support doubles". If they do, you have early distributional information at your disposal.

| West | North | East | South (you) |
|------|-------|------|-------------|
| 1♦   | pass  | 1♠   | 2♣          |

Playing support doubles, a double of two clubs shows three card spade support, a raise to two spades shows four spades, bidding another suit or passing denies three spades. If your two club bid should happen to end the auction, play West for fewer than three spades.

142. When RHO fails to double a high level cue-bid or a Blackwood response for the lead, assume LHO has the important missing honor(s) in the suit.

143. When you have five cards between your hand and dummy in a major that has been bid once, assume a 5-3 division. If the suit was divided 4-4, it would have been supported; if the suit was divided 6-2, it would have been rebid.

144. Remember, everybody doesn't bid as beautifully or as accurately as you do. You must make allowances in your inferences depending upon the skill level of your opponents.

# CHAPTER 8

# PLAY INFERENCES

145. When the dummy comes down with a threatening side suit yet the opponents adopt a passive defense, you can bet the house and lot that either the side suit or the trump suit is not breaking well for you.

146. If the opponents adopt an active defense when dummy has a threatening side suit, assume the side suit is breaking evenly.

147. If a player does not make an obvious play, he probably has a key honor from which he fears leading.

148. If a GOOD defender gives you an entry to dummy where none existed, he is probably tempting you to take a losing finesse. It is a common ploy for a defender holding the singleton king of trump behind declarer to go out of his way to put you in dummy.

149. When an accurate defender signals encouragement with a high spot card, he denies the spot card directly above. Therefore if RHO signals with an eight spot, he denies the nine.

150. Opponents' mannerisms, however inadvertent, give away a certain amount of gratuitous information. Keep your antennae extended.

151. Eventually your job is to construct possible hands the defenders might hold to justify either their bidding, their defensive plays or both. After you come up with a possible hand, ask yourself these questions: (1) if the opponent has this hand, would the bidding have been the same? (2) Would the defense have been the same? If the answer to either question is "no", back to the drawing board. Try to come up with a different hand that will give you a "yes" answer to both questions.

152. If the opponents create a finesse position where none could have logically existed, DO NOT take the finesse.

```
                    North (dummy)
                    K1076
     West                              East
     ?J9                               8?
                    South (you)
                    A5432
```

You lead the ace, West plays the jack and East the eight. When you lead low towards dummy, West plays the nine. Play the king. West cannot have the queen. With QJ9, West would not have played the jack originally.

153. Be ever so wary of this swindle position:

**North** (dummy)
J65

**West**
?

**East**
?

**South** (you)
K3

At some time during the defense of a suit contract, East leads a low card in this side suit. Assume you can only afford to lose one trick. If East has led from the queen, you should play low. On the other hand if East has led from the ace, you should play the king. What to do?

If there is NO REASON for East to lead this suit (no discards available from any other suit), play the KING. Holding the queen, East can sit back and wait for his two tricks. If discards are available and East must attack the suit, put on your guessing cap.

154. If a defender declines to ruff one of your winners, he is either void in trump or has a strong trump holding which he does not want to weaken. Usually it is the latter.

155. When the defenders do not make an obvious play, there must be an obvious reason.

**North** (dummy)
♠ A2
♥ 3
♦ AK765
♣ AKJ87

**South** (you)
♠ KJ10943
♥ 876
♦ 32
♣ Q4

After you open a Weak Two in spades, partner sets you down gently in six spades. West leads the ♥K. East overtakes and returns the ♦Q. What do you make of all this and who has the ♠Q?

If either defender had ♠Qxx, a simple heart continuation, forcing dummy to trump ensures a defensive trump trick. Why didn't they do this? Because the queen of spades is doubleton and they want you to finesse. Don't play into their hands. Plunk down the ♠AK and pick off somebody's doubleton queen.

# CHAPTER 9

# LOWER MATHEMATICS

In order to be a good bridge player you do not have to know all the percentages. If you are familiar with the likelihoods of the common suit divisions and you use a little common sense, the following tips should be enough.

156. The three most common distributional hand patterns are 4-4-3-2, 5-3-3-2 and 5-4-3-1 in that order. Together they comprise 50% of all hand patterns; throw in 4-3-3-3 and 5-4-2-2 and you are up to 71%.

157. Because you usually attack long suits first, you should be familiar with how THEIR cards are most apt to be divided in your long suits.

158. When you have seven cards between your hand and dummy, expect their cards to divide 4-2 48% of the time and 3-3 36% of the time. This tip may come in handy when you find yourself playing, heaven forbid, a seven card trump fit.

159. When you have eight cards between your hand and the dummy, expect a 3-2 break 68% of the time and a 4-1 break 28% of the time.

160. When you have nine cards between your hand and the dummy, expect a 3-1 break 50%, a 2-2 break 40% and a 4-0 break 10% of the time.

161. When you have 10 cards between your hand and the dummy, expect a 2-1 break 78% and a 3-0 break 22% of the time.

162. What does it all mean? It means that when the opponents have an even number of cards between them (say, six), those six cards are more apt to be divided unevenly, (4-2) than evenly (3-3).

163. When the opponents have an odd number of cards assume those cards will break as evenly as possible. If the opponents have five cards, assume a 3-2 division. If the opponents have seven cards, assume a 4-3 division.

164. With ten trumps between your hand and dummy missing the king, take the finesse. However if you can throw in an opponent with the king to force a losing return, play the ace.

**North** (dummy)
♠ QJ1043
♥ A72
♦ K4
♣ A76

**South** (you)
♠ A9876
♥ K3
♦ A75
♣ KJ10

Say you are playing six spades with the ♥Q lead. Considering the spades in ISOLATION, the best play is a finesse. But, looking at the hand in total, the best play is the ACE. Even if the king does not drop, you can strip the red suits and exit a trump forcing a club play. If your clubs were Kxx, take the trump finesse.

165. A finesse in one suit is more likely than a 3-3 break in another suit.

**North** (dummy)
♠ AQ
♥ 543
♦ A765
♣ 5432

**South** (you)
♠ 872
♥ J96
♦ KQ3
♣ AKQJ

You wind up in 3NT and West leads a low heart from K10xx. The opponents take the first four heart tricks and West shifts to a spade. You have eight sure tricks with a possible ninth in either spades or diamonds. Unfortunately, you have not had a chance to test the diamonds. West has put it to you. Take the spade finesse, a 50% shot, rather than hoping diamonds divide 3-3, a 36% play.

166. A 3-2 break in one suit is far more likely than a successful finesse in another suit. (68% vs. 50%)

**North** (dummy)
♠ AQ
♥ 543
♦ A7653
♣ 543

**South** (you)
♠ 952
♥ J106
♦ KQ2
♣ AKQJ

33

Against your 3NT, the opponents cash four hearts and lead a spade through your AQ. This time decline the finesse. A 3-2 break in diamonds (68%) is better than the 50-50 spade finesse.

167. No matter how forlorn an opponent looks, do not play him for a complete yarborough (no card higher than a nine). The chances of that happening are one in 1827!

168. There is a 4 to 1 likelihood that on any given hand at least one player will either have a singleton or a void. Let's hope that it is not your partner who has one in your long suit.

169. When you are missing an important honor and you know how that suit is divided, assume the player with the greater length has the honor. The fact that the player with the greater length discards several cards from that suit does NOT change the odds.

170. When you are missing ONE important honor originally and arrive at a position where the opponents remain with two cards, including the important honor, play for the drop.

**North** (dummy)
KJ874

**West**
?

**East**
?

**South** (you)
A632

You begin with the ace and both follow. At this point the opponents remain with two cards; one important, the queen. When you lead low, West plays the ten. Play for the drop, rise with the king.

171. Say you are missing TWO important cards in the same suit and as you play the suit one of them appears. When you finally arrive at a position where the opponents have two cards remaining in the suit, finesse for the other important card.

**North** (dummy)
KQ94

**West**

**East**

**South** (you)
A32

Before you attack this combination you should notice that two important cards are missing, the ten and the jack. Say you begin by leading low to the king and then low to the ace, East playing either the ten or the jack on the second round. On the third round of the suit percentages dictate that you lead low to the nine.

172. A similar situation:

**North** (dummy)
K1043

**West**                        **East**
                                  J or Q

**South** (you)
A8765

You lead the ace and East plays either the jack or the queen; one of the TWO important missing cards. At this point the opponents remain with two cards, one important, one not. Take the finesse. Lead low to the ten.

173. When three important cards are missing originally and two have appeared, with two cards remaining take a finesse for the third missing important card.

**North** (dummy)
♠ AQ83

**West**                           **East**

**South** (you)
♠ K42

Because you have the eight in dummy and a later finesse may be available, the jack, ten and nine are all important cards. When you lead low to the ace and then low to the king, East produces the J10, J9 or 109. At this point two cards remain; one of them is important. Lead low to the eight on your return trip.

The above tips assume you do not have a count in the suit. With the count, you will know what to do in these two card endings.

174. A little over 50% of the hands either you or your opponents hold will have between 7 and 12 HCP. I know, I know, you have all the 7 pointers.

175. If you hold a five card suit, there is a roughly a 30% chance that your partner has exactly three cards in that suit.

176. If you hold a four card suit, there is a 22% chance that your partner also holds exactly four cards in the suit. (One of the reasons to use Stayman).

# CHAPTER 10

# PLACING THE CARDS

Successful declarers "know" where the missing honors are. How do they know? Read on.

177. The simplest technique of card placing is to listen to the bidding. Silence can be more revealing than noise.

178. An original pass is very informative. Play an opponent who passes originally for FEWER than 12 HCP.

179. If a player who passes originally turns up with 10 cards in two suits, amend "Fewer than 12 HCP" to fewer than 11 HCP.

180. When a passed hand makes a takeout double assume 9-11 HCP. Don't call the cops if it turns out to be one fewer.

181. Assume an opening bidder has at least 12 HCP. However if the opener turns up with a distributional hand, he may have as few as 10-11 HCP. Do not assume fewer than 10 HCP.

182. Play close attention to the high cards that each defender produces as the play develops. You may be able to tie in this information with the bidding to locate other honors.

183. If a passed hand begins the defense by leading the AK of a suit, assume no other missing ace in that hand. If the same player later turns up with a queen, assume no other missing king or queen in that hand.

184. If a passed hand begins the defense by leading the AKQ of a suit, you have just seen Paris. Play RHO for the other aces and kings.

185. If an opponent opens one club, never makes another peep and turns up with a three card club suit, several inferences are available: (1) opener has a balanced hand with no side five card suit; (2) opener was either too weak or too strong to open one notrump—probably too weak given the bidding; (3) opener is either 4-4 in the majors or 4-3-3-3, the four card suit a MAJOR.

**North** (dummy)
♠ AJ3
♥ A765
♦ K54
♣ 765

**South** (you)
♠ K105
♥ QJ109
♦ AQ6
♣ 982

After West opens 1♣, you find yourself playing four hearts. West leads three top clubs (9HCP), East follows high-low showing an even number, obviously four. At trick four West shifts to the ♦J (10HCP) which you win in your hand to finesse in hearts. It turns out West has ♥Kxx. (13 HCP). Who has the ♠Q? It depends upon their notrump range. If the range is 15-17, play East for the queen. If the range is 16-18, you cannot be sure.

186.   A time proven technique for locating a missing important honor is to drive out a non-important honor first. This may tell you who has the important honor.

**North** (dummy)
♠ AJ104
♥ QJ1043
♦ 764
♣ J

**South** (you)
♠ K987
♥ 2
♦ QJ3
♣ KQ1098

| West | North | East | South |
|------|-------|------|-------|
| Pass | Pass | Pass | 1♣ |
| Pass | 1♥ | Pass | 1♠ |
| Pass | 3♠ | All Pass | |

Opening lead: ♥K (King from Ace-King)

West shifts to the ♦10 at trick two and East plays the king, ace and a third diamond to your queen. Who has the ♠Q?

At this point you can't tell. Each defender has passed originally and each has turned up with 7 HCP. The trick is to knock out the ace of clubs. Whoever has that card will have started with 11 HCP. Clearly, the ♠Q will be in the other hand.

187. You can even use this technique to ferret out a jack! If each passed hand defender has turned up with 7HCP and you are missing an unimportant ace and an important jack, knock out the ace and play the partner for the jack.

188. The more common scenarios have you missing an important queen and an unimportant king or vice versa. Locate the unimportant honor first and play the partner for the important one. Do the same when you are missing two queens, one important and one not.

189. In the real world, you don't always have time to discover who has what. Enter the world of positive and negative assumptions.

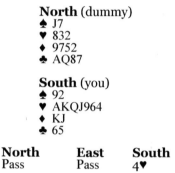

**North** (dummy)
♠ J7
♥ 832
♦ 9752
♣ AQ87

**South** (you)
♠ 92
♥ AKQJ964
♦ KJ
♣ 65

| West | North | East | South |
|------|-------|------|-------|
| Pass | Pass | Pass | 4♥ |
| All Pass | | | |

Opening lead: ♠K

At trick two West leads a low spade to East's ace and East returns a low diamond. Which diamond should you play?

There are several factors involved. First, look at the entire hand before making your diamond play. Consider your club suit. In order to make this hand West must have the ♣K. Assume West has it!

WHEN YOU NEED A PARTICULAR CARD IN A PARTICULAR HAND AND HAVE NOT HAD TIME TO FIND OUT WHETHER IT IS THERE OR NOT, ASSUME IT IS THERE AND SEE IF THAT DOESN'T HELP YOU LOCATE OTHER HONORS.

If West has the ♣K (positive assumption necessary to make the hand) along with the ♠KQ (8HCP), he cannot have the ♦A or else he would have opened the bidding. If the hand is makeable, East must have the ♦A. Play the king.

190. The other side of the coin is the negative assumption. When things look bleak, make positive assumptions. When things look rosy, make negative assumptions.

**North** (dummy)
- ♠ AQ63
- ♥ 10432
- ♦ 432
- ♣ KQ

**South** (you)
- ♠ 75
- ♥ AKQ987
- ♦ KJ
- ♣ 532

You open one heart in fourth seat and wind up in four hearts against silent opponents. West leads the ♣10 to East's ace and East returns the dreaded low diamond. What should you do?

You should stop and think! Before sweating over which diamond to play, consider the entire hand. If the spade finesse works, you are always cold and your diamond play is simply for an overtrick.

It is only if the spade finesse is wrong that you must get the diamonds right. Assume it is wrong! If East has the ♠K to go along with his known ♣AJ from the lead, East can hardly have the ♦A (12 HCP) or else he would have opened the bidding.

If East cannot have the ♦A, West must have it. (Brilliant!) Play the ♦J in hopes of driving out West's "known" ace. If West wins the ♦Q and returns a diamond to East's ace, do NOT burn this book! West will have the ♠K.

191. When responder passes his partner's MAJOR suit opening bid (in the absence of competition), assume responder has fewer than 6HCP.

192. When responder passes his partner's MINOR suit opening bid (in the absence of competition), assume fewer than 4-5 HCP. Most responders will bend over backwards to respond one heart or one spade to a minor suit opening with 4-5 HCP, particularly with a five card suit or longer.

193. Placing or finding important cards is tied in with counting— points and distribution.

**North** (dummy)
K109

**South** (you)
Q87

You need two tricks from the suit and must broach the suit. Whom should you play for the jack? The opponent who has it. Just kidding.

With no honor information to go by, play the opponent who is likely to be LONGER in the suit for the jack.

However if there has been revealing bidding, you may be able to pick off that jack. Assume RHO has opened a 15-17 notrump and has shown up with 14 HCP in the three other suits. Voila, RHO has the jack and LHO has the ace.

194. Knowing third hand plays the LOWER OR LOWEST of equals allows you to place all or most of the missing honors in the suit that has been led.

**North** (dummy)
76

**West**
2

**East**
K

**South** (you)
A104

West leads the deuce against a SUIT contract and East plays the king. Who has what? Surely West has the queen, but what about the jack? Play East for the jack. With QJxx the normal lead is the queen. Versus notrump the location of the jack would be a mystery.

195. 
**North** (dummy)
76

**West**
2

**East**
K

**South** (you)
1053

Versus a suit contract, West leads the deuce and East plays the king. What is going on? East must have the ace (aces are not normally underled vs. suit). West must have the queen (East's play of the king has denied the queen) and East must have the jack as well. With the queen and the jack West would have led the queen. Visualize West with Qxxx and East with AKJx. If East is a passed hand, play West for any missing ace and more likely than not any missing king.

196. Allow for 10-11 point non-vulnerable opening bids in third seat particularly in tournament play.

197. Dramatic plays are available when you know who has what.

**North** (dummy)
765

**West**
K9

**East**
J108

**South** (you)
AQ432

If West is marked with the king, lead the ace and then low hoping the king is either singleton or doubleton.

198. Knowing that an ace will seldom be underled at trick ONE turns guesses into near certainties.

**North** (dummy)
KJ4

**West**
Q1065

**East**
A872

**South** (you)
93

West leads low. As you "know" East has the ace, play the jack. However if you need TWO tricks from this suit, play LOW and hope West has led from the Q10. Sometimes East will have the A10xx and play the ace. Even if East plays the ten, you can later lead low to the jack and establish the king for a discard.

199. Experienced declarers never go wrong in this position:

**North** (dummy)
AJ6

**West**
Q1065

**East**
K875

**South** (you)
92

If West leads low on the go vs. a suit contract, East is marked with at least one honor in the suit so there is no point in playing the jack. Play low. If West has led from honor-ten, East must spend his honor. Later you can lead low to the jack if necessary. At notrump play the same.

200. When there can be no material advantage in playing an honor from dummy, play low and put pressure on third hand. Reread this one.

**North** (dummy)
Q76

**West**
KJ82

**East**
A1094

**South** (you)
53

Once again a small card is led vs. suit. Play low. IT'S NOT WHAT YOU HAVE, IT'S WHAT THEY FEAR YOU MAY HAVE. In the diagram position East has to make the potentially dangerous play of the nine to prevent you from eventually taking a trick with the queen.

201. You cannot draw the same lead inferences about the location of the adverse honors once the dummy has been tabled. Defenders are more apt to underlead aces or KQ combinations AFTER they can see the dummy.

202. Most defenders play that the lead of a low card promises an honor. If they do, more honor placement becomes possible.

**North** (dummy)
KQ6

**West**
x

**East**

**South** (you)
102

Assume a low card is led vs. a suit contract. You can place the ace with East, but where is the jack? If a low card lead shows an honor, West has it. If you need two tricks in the suit, play low.

203. One is never too thrilled to have an opponent lead through a KJ combination. However when the player playing AFTER the KJ has the setting tricks in another suit, play the king.

**North** (dummy)
♠ 87
♥ 8743
♦ AQJ107
♣ AJ

**South** (you)
♠ A104
♥ KJ10
♦ 982
♣ KQ105

You wind up in a routine 3NT and West leads the ♠3. East plays the king which you duck. You also duck East's return of the nine. West continues a third spade driving out the ace. Visualize ♠QJxxx with West and ♠K9x with East.

At trick four you run the nine of diamonds to East's king. East returns the inevitable low heart. This time there is NO guess. If West—with the setting tricks in spades—has the ♥A, you cannot make the hand. Play East for the ♥A. Rise with the king.

204. Beware of Greeks bearing gifts. If a good player suddenly gives you a chance for a finesse that you cannot take for yourself, forget the finesse and play for the drop. If a weak player makes the same play, you've got problems.

**North** (dummy)
K76

**West**
10 or J10

**East**
A5 or AJ5

**South** (you)
Q98432

This is your trump suit and dummy has no side entry. You lead low to the king and ace, West playing the ten. At this point East returns the five. Should you finesse? Only if East has the I.Q. of a tree. With AJx, East can return another suit. Why would East give you a free finesse? Don't join the tree people, play the queen.

205. Normal looking plays must at times be altered if the bidding has tipped you off that something is "up".

South-North vul.
DealerNorth

**North** (dummy)
♠ 3
♥ KJ1098
♦ KQ4
♣ KQJ10

**West**
♠ 92
♥ Q753
♦ 10952
♣ 976

**East**
♠ QJ108765
♥ A64
♦ A
♣ 53

**South** (you)
♠ AK4
♥ 2
♦ J8763
♣ A842

| North | East | South | West |
|-------|------|-------|------|
| 1♥ | 1♠ | 2♦ | Pass |
| 3♦ | 3♠ | 3NT | Pass |
| Pass | Pass | | |

Opening lead: ♣9

With East marked with seven spades from the lead and both red aces from the bidding, the normal play of winning the second spade and leading a low diamond may not work. East may have a singleton ace. Cross to dummy with a club and lead a low diamond. If diamonds are 3-2, both plays work.

206. Listen to the bidding, watch the opening lead, follow the honors that each hand produces, make inferences from their plays, and blame everything that goes wrong on your partner. Once you master all of these techniques, you will have "arrived".

# CHAPTER 11

# BELOVED FINESSES

There is nothing dearer to the heart of the average player than taking a finesse. Whereas the expert will move heaven and earth to avoid one, the non-expert cannot take them fast enough. Read on carefully if you have finesseaholic tendencies.

207. Finesses, particularly in short suits, are last resort measures. The idea is to either avoid taking them altogether, or at least postpone taking them until the last possible moment.

208. Try to establish long suits before taking finesses in short suits.

209. With a choice of two finesses—one in a long suit, one in a short suit—take the long suit finesse first. With the long suit established, you may not need the short suit finesse.

210. Do not play by nursery rhymes (eight ever-nine never) when dealing with eight or nine card suits missing the queen. There are usually other factors involved. When no other factors are involved, play by rhymes.

211. The most frequent reason to finesse into one hand or the other with nine cards missing the queen is to keep the dangerous hand off lead.

**North** (dummy)
♠ K642
♥ 432
♦ AJ754
♣ A

**South** (you)
♠ AJ753
♥ K65
♦ KQ9
♣ 65

Your contract is four spades and West leads a club. If you look only at spades, you will play the AK hoping the Q drops. But if you look at the whole hand, you will see that East is the danger hand since he can lead a heart through your king. In order to keep East off play, finesse the spade into West. Even if the finesse loses, you can still discard two hearts on the diamonds and never have to suffer a possible "heart attack" from East.

212. No matter how much fun it is to take finesses, do not take two finesses when you need only one.

44

**North** (dummy)
- ♠ QJ105
- ♥ 1052
- ♦ AQJ3
- ♣ J2

**South** (you)
- ♠ AK9876
- ♥ J43
- ♦ 65
- ♣ AQ

You wind up in four spades and West leads the king, queen and a third heart to East's Ace. East shifts to a club. Play the ace! You do not need the club finesse, you need the diamond finesse! If the diamond finesse works, you can repeat the finesse and discard your queen of clubs. If the diamond finesse fails, the hand cannot be made.

213. Do not overlook seemingly remote chances to drop stray honors before taking a finesse.

**North** (dummy)
- ♠ J32
- ♥ AQJ4
- ♦ AQ5
- ♣ QJ10

**South** (you)
- ♠ AK
- ♥ K109876
- ♦ 32
- ♣ 876

You get to four hearts and West leads the king, ace and a third club, East ruffing. East exits with a spade. After drawing trump, it can't hurt to cash a second spade just in case the queen drops. If it doesn't, take the diamond finesse.

214. At times a finesse can be avoided by establishing an honor card in another suit.

**North** (dummy)
- ♠ AJ98
- ♥ Q543
- ♦ A76
- ♣ 32

**South** (you)
- ♠ KQ7654
- ♥ J
- ♦ KJ2
- ♣ AK4

Your beautiful bidding gets you to six spades and West leads the ♥A and shifts to a club. Before even thinking of taking the diamond finesse, trump a couple of hearts...the king may drop.

215. When you have a side suit that is equally divided between your hand and dummy, you have a potential throw-in suit. Even if this side suit has a finesse option, it might be safer to give up on the finesse and use the suit as a throw-in suit.

**North** (dummy)
♠ AQ
♥ J109
♦ 87654
♣ J54

**South** (you)
♠ J10
♥ 876
♦ AKQ9
♣ A1032

You steal the hand for two diamonds and West leads the king and a low heart to East's ace. East returns a heart to West's queen and West exits with a low spade. If you look only at spades, you will surely take the finesse. But, if you look at the whole hand, you will see that you do not need the spade finesse. Win the ♠A, draw trump and exit with a spade forcing the opponents to broach clubs. With the hand stripped, the most you can lose is one club trick.

216. Two chances are better than one. With two finesses available in a position where you can only afford to lose one trick, take the finesse which, if it loses, will still allow you to take the other one.

**North** (dummy)
♠ 4
♥ 54
♦ AQJ653
♣ K1087

**South** (you)
♠ K73
♥ AQJ10
♦ K1098
♣ A3

You wind up in six diamonds and West leads a passive trump, East following. Lead up to the king of spades. If East has the ace, you will not need the heart finesse. If West has the ace, you still have the heart finesse to fall back on. If you take the heart finesse first and it loses, the opponents will cash the ♠A and school is out.

217. With two finesses available and a queen missing in each suit, you might have to combine your chances. If you cannot afford to lose a trick, play the AK of the longer suit. If the queen does not drop, take a finesse in the shorter suit.

**North** (dummy)
♠ AJ43
♥ 98
♦ AQ32
♣ K43

**South** (you)
♠ K52
♥ K5
♦ K76
♣ AJ765

Your contract is 3NT and West leads the ♥4. East wins the ace and returns the jack.

You have eight top tricks and you can't afford to give up the lead. First play on diamonds. If they do not divide 3-3, you must fall back on your black suits.

Play the ♣AK, the longer suit, and if the queen does not appear, cash the ♠K and lead low to the ♠J taking a finesse in the shorter suit.

218. If a suit is led in which dummy is void facing a king in your hand, you might be able to avoid a finesse in another suit by discarding from dummy.

**North** (dummy)
♠ AQ4
♥ −
♦ KJ8764
♣ AJ76

**South** (you)
♠ 632
♥ K98
♦ AQ10932
♣ 4

You get to a fabulous six diamond contract and West leads the ♥Q. Rather than fret about spades, discard a spade from dummy. After East wins the Ace, discard the ♠Q on the king of hearts. You lose one heart, but no spades.

219. When a suit is led in which dummy is void and you have QJx(x) in your hand along with several "slow losers", discard a loser from dummy. Later run the queen through the opening leader in order to establish the jack to discard another loser.

**North** (dummy)
♠ A98
♥ —
♦ KJ8764
♣ 9876

**West**
♠ K54
♥ K1032
♦ 92
♣ KJ32

**East**
♠ QJ32
♥ A9864
♦ 5
♣ Q105

**South** (you)
♠ 1076
♥ QJ75
♦ AQ103
♣ A4

You get to five diamonds and West leads a low heart. If you ruff, you wind up losing three tricks in the blacks. If you discard a spade from dummy and later run the ♥Q through West, you can discard a second spade upon the ♥J. All you need is to find the ♥K with West. Better than zilch.

220. "Practice finesses" are for novices. The definition of a practice finesse is a finesse which, if it wins, gains you nothing; if it loses, it costs you the contract.

**North** (dummy)
♠ AQJ
♥ 432
♦ 876
♣ KQJ3

**South** (you)
♠ 743
♥ AKQJ10
♦ KQJ
♣ A8

You wind up in six hearts and West leads a low spade. Finessing the spade at trick one is the perfect example of a practice finesse. If it works, you take twelve tricks; if it doesn't, down you go. If you don't take the finesse, you also have twelve tricks but no risk. Draw trump, discard two spades on the clubs and concede the ♦A.

221. When an opponent leads a high card through an AQx combination and you have xxx or xxxx in the opposite hand, it is not against the law to play the ace! You can always lead up to the queen later. With a little bit of luck, you may not have to.

48

**North** (dummy)
♠ KQJ
♥ AQ5
♦ 5
♣ J109874

**South** (you)
♠ 32
♥ 876
♦ A42
♣ AK532

You get to five clubs and West leads the ♥J. There is no need to finesse the queen. If it loses and a heart comes back, you stand a good chance of losing two hearts and a spade.

Win the Ace of hearts, draw trumps and knock out the ♠A. If EAST has the Ace, you are home free. East cannot attack your ♥Q and you can discard a heart on a spade. If West has the ♠A and leads a second heart, play the queen. You still survive if West started with the ♥K or East a doubleton king.

222. Do not overlook the element of "time". Time refers to how many times you can afford to let the opponents in before you have no time left to make your contract!

**North** (dummy)
♠ 10987
♥ A32
♦ Q4
♣ A876

**South** (you)
♠ KQJ65
♥ K54
♦ KJ7
♣ 32

You get to four spades and West leads the ♥Q. With a loser in each suit you must develop the diamonds for a heart pitch. The key is to notice that you do not have "time" to drive out the ♠A. The opponents can win and play a second heart. Upon getting in with the ♦A they will cash the setting trick in hearts.

You must play diamonds BEFORE spades. Even then you must take care to preserve an entry to your hand in case the opponents win the second diamond. Win the ♥A in DUMMY and drive out the ♦A. Win the likely heart return and discard a heart from dummy on a winning diamond. Now you have TIME to drive out the ♠A.

If your diamonds were K10x, you would also have to attack diamonds before spades intending to finesse the ten after the ace was driven out.

49

223. With a two-way finesse for a queen in the trump suit, it may be right not to finesse either way!

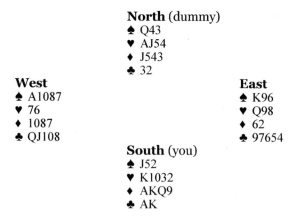

**North** (dummy)
- ♠ Q43
- ♥ AJ54
- ♦ J543
- ♣ 32

**West**
- ♠ A1087
- ♥ 76
- ♦ 1087
- ♣ QJ108

**East**
- ♠ K96
- ♥ Q98
- ♦ 62
- ♣ 97654

**South** (you)
- ♠ J52
- ♥ K1032
- ♦ AKQ9
- ♣ AK

After you open 2NT, partner Staymans you into four hearts. West leads the ♣Q. Along with the dreaded mirrored distribution (identical distribution in each hand), you have a possible trump loser and three possible spade losers. However, if you can force the OPPONENTS to lead spades... Win the club and play the ace-king of hearts. Assume the queen does not drop. Cash a second club and then run the diamonds. If East ruffs, a favorable return must be made. If East doesn't ruff, throw East in with a trump and force a favorable return.

224. If the opponents lead through an honor combination in the dummy facing a void in your hand, you have a chance to take a "free" finesse.

**North** (dummy)
- ♠ AKJ10
- ♥ 32
- ♦ KJ7
- ♣ KJ98

**South** (you)
- ♠ —
- ♥ AQ54
- ♦ Q108
- ♣ AQ10432

You arrive at six clubs and West leads a spade. Play the jack. If East covers, ruff and later pitch three hearts on the established spades. If the jack holds, you also get three heart pitches. If the dummy had AKJx in spades, it would still be right to play the jack. If it is covered, fall back on the heart finesse. If the jack holds, you will not need the heart finesse.

225. When you have a nine card trump fit missing the queen and one opponent has preempted, play the preemptor's partner for the queen.

**North** (dummy)
A1043

**West**                                           **East**

**South** (you)
KJ987

This is your trump suit. If West has preempted, play East for the queen. If East has preempted, play West for the queen.

226. If the bidding tells you that a finesse can't possibly succeed, don't take it. Play for the drop instead.

**North** (dummy)
♠ AQ32
♥ QJ
♦ KJ1052
♣ 102

**South** (you)
♠ J107654
♥ K9
♦ AQ4
♣ QJ

After West passes originally, you become declarer at four spades. West leads the king-ace of clubs and then the ace and a heart. As West has already shown up with 11 HCP, West cannot have the ♠K. Play for the drop instead. Who knows? The Rabbi's Rule might work here. The Rabbi's Rule: When the king is singleton, play the ace.

227. Advanced tip. With a choice of two finesses, one suit missing a queen, the other a king and you can't afford to lose a trick, play the high card(s) in the suit where an honor is more likely to drop. If the honor doesn't drop, take a finesse in the other suit.

**North** (dummy)
♠ AQ5
♥ A87
♦ KJ1043
♣ 65

**South** (you)
♠ 4
♥ KQJ1032
♦ A65
♣ KQ2

You arrive at six hearts and West leads a club to East's Ace. East returns a club. You have a possible diamond loser. Should you take the diamond finesse or the spade finesse? Give yourself two chances. Draw trump and play the AK of diamonds, the suit in which one of the missing honors is more likely to drop. If the queen does not appear, take the spade finesse.

228. With a side suit singleton facing the AQJ in a trump contract, you have options. If you need to develop an extra trick: (1) Lead low to the queen, (2) lead to the ace and run the queen if not covered. When there is a danger hand involved, your choice is simple. Do NOT finesse into the danger hand!

**North** (dummy)
♠ J10542
♥ AQJ
♦ 432
♣ KQ

**South** (you)
♠ AKQ876
♥ 2
♦ K87
♣ 876

You wind up in four spades and West leads the ace and a club. Your problem is diamonds and East is the danger hand because he alone can lead THROUGH the king. To avoid this unpleasant prospect, draw trump and lead a heart to the ace followed by the queen (a ruffing finesse). Either the queen will: (1) win and you will have avoided losing three diamond tricks, (2) lose and you will have a diamond discard available on the ♥J, or (3) be covered and ruffed, setting up a diamond discard on the ♥J. In the meantime, East is still waiting to get in to push a diamond through your king.

229. The more likely reason to take a ruffing finesse rather than a simple finesse is to rid yourself of an immediate loser, intending to rid yourself of an eventual loser later.

**North** (dummy)
♠ A65
♥ AQJ
♦ K1098
♣ A54

**South** (you)
♠ 732
♥ 2
♦ AQJ765
♣ K32

After a bidding misunderstanding, (partner's fault of course) you wind up in five diamonds instead of 3NT. West leads a spade.

In order to assure your contract, win the ♠A, draw trumps, cross to the ace of hearts and run the queen, discarding a spade if East plays low. Assume West wins. You have one remaining loser, a spade. Your ♥J will take care of your club loser. You make the hand regardless of who has the ♥K. If you lead a low heart to the queen, down you go if East has "his majesty".

230. Be aware of the possibility of a "backward" finesse when a "frontward" finesse cannot possibly work.

**North** (dummy)
K32

**West**
Q876

**East**
1054

**South** (you)
AJ9

If the bidding has absolutely marked West with the queen and there is little or no chance that it is doubleton, lead the jack. If West covers, win the king and finesse the nine on the way back.

231. When contemplating a "backward" finesse, if the nine is NOT in the same hand with the AJ or the KJ, the PARTNERSHIP must have both the eight and the nine to compensate.

**North** (dummy)
K98

**West**
Q432

**East**
1076

**South** (you)
AJ5

If you are sure West has the queen, lead the jack. If it is covered, win the king and run the nine. Without the eight this play won't work. (East covers the nine).

232. Some "backward" finesses are more impressive than others. If you ever pull this one off, go straight to the head of the class.

**North** (dummy)
K43

**West**
AJ6

**East**
9752

**South** (you)
Q108

Assume you need two tricks from this combination and you know from the bidding that West has both missing honors. Lead the ten. If West plays low, so do you. If West covers with the jack, win the king and lead low to the eight. Applause.

233. If the entry situation to the long suit is acute, don't waste entries to take risky finesses.

**North** (dummy)
♠ 73
♥ AK7
♦ 1096543
♣ 65

**South** (you)
♠ AK8
♥ 532
♦ AQ2
♣ AK43

The contract is 3NT. The lead is the ♣2. The idea, of course, is to set up the diamonds. Win the ♣K and play the ♦AQ. Do not waste a heart entry to take the diamond finesse. Terrible things can happen to you if the finesse loses and a heart comes back. If the diamonds don't break, what is to become of you?

234. Even though a simple finesse in one suit (50%) offers a better chance for an extra trick than playing for a 3-3 break in another suit (36%), best of all is to combine both plays (68%).

**North** (dummy)
♠ QJ3
♥ 43
♦ A876
♣ AK32

**South** (you)
♠ AK4
♥ AKJ
♦ K32
♣ QJ54

6NT is your resting place and the lead is the ♠10. You have 11 top tricks with a chance for twelve in either diamonds (3-3 division) or a heart finesse. Try both. Duck a diamond. When you regain the lead, test the diamonds. If they are not 3-3, fall back on the heart finesse. If you take the heart finesse first (another kindergarten play) and it loses, you cannot test the diamonds.

One lady in my class has taken the losing heart finesse ten years in a row without testing diamonds. (In my class diamonds are 3-3 and the heart finesse doesn't work. Next year I am giving East the ♥Q. I can't stand it any more).

235. When you have to choose which finesse to take between two suits each missing the king, play the ace of the longer suit. If the king does not drop, take a finesse in the shorter suit. (The same technique you use when missing two queens).

**North** (dummy)
♠ A2
♥ KQ43
♦ AQ76
♣ A65

**South** (you)
♠ QJ109876
♥ A
♦ 2
♣ 9874

You wind up in six spades and West leads the ♣K. Grab your ace, cross to the ♥A and tempt West with the ♠Q. (ALWAYS give them a chance to cover an honor with an honor). If West does not play the king, rise with the ace, discard two clubs on the hearts, ruff a heart back to your hand and take the diamond finesse. Of course you could look like a fool if West had ♠Kx and three hearts. Such is life when you play the percentages.

236. Say you are missing two kings in finesseable suits, one a singleton facing an AQ combination, the other a doubleton facing an AQJ combination and you cannot afford to lose the trick. First try to ruff out the king in the singleton suit. If that doesn't work, take the finesse in the doubleton suit.

**North** (dummy)
♠ 765
♥ AQ65
♦ AQJ
♣ 1098

**South** (you)
♠ K43
♥ 3
♦ 42
♣ AKQJ765

Your contract is five clubs and West leads the ♠2. East wins the ace and returns the jack. Rather than put all your eggs in one basket by taking either red suit finesse, give yourself two chances. Play the ace and ruff a heart. Assuming nothing dramatic has happened, return to dummy with a trump and ruff a second heart. If the king has not appeared, take the diamond finesse.

237. Do not forget about desperation finesses.

**North** (dummy)
Q10

**South** (you)
AK32

If you need four tricks from this suit, lead low to the ten. Play the same if dummy has K10 or A10 and you have AQxx or KQxx.

238. Along with the fake finesse, the ruffing finesse, the desperation finesse and the backward finesse, let's not forget the intra finesse.

**North** (dummy)
Q82

**West**
J3

**East**
K10765

**South** (you)
A94

If the bidding has marked East with the king plus length,lead low to the eight.

Later lead the queen hoping to pin the ten or jack thus establishing the NINE.

239.

**North** (dummy)
J973

**West**
105

**East**
KQ2

**South** (you)
A864

This might be your trump suit in a slam contract! Lead low to the nine and if it drives out an honor, cross to dummy and lead the jack and hope to blot out the doubleton ten in the West hand.

Both of these intra finesses require the eight and the nine to be held by the declaring side.

240. You can pick up oodles of extra tricks by tempting players to cover an honor with an honor even though you are NOT planning to finesse.

**North** (dummy)
A43

**West**
Q6

**East**
872

**South** (you)
KJ1095

Perhaps your intention is to play East for the queen. Instead of leading the five to the ace and then taking the finesse, lead the JACK to the ace. You will be pleasantly surprised how often the jack is covered.

Caution! You must have the necessary missing spot cards to attack with an honor that you are planning to overtake. In this example you could not afford to lead the jack if you did not have the nine. (A 4-1 break would do you in).

241. Don't overlook the opportunity to give your opponents fits in this common position:

**North** (dummy)
J43

**South** (you)
K10

If you can only afford to lose one trick in this suit, try leading the jack from dummy. It often coaxes the queen. If the queen is not played, there is good reason to believe that East does not have the queen.

242. When you have a CONCEALED suit, you can almost bet that when you lead an honor from dummy in that suit, second hand will cover. If second hand does not cover, play fourth hand for the missing honor.

**North** (dummy)
J4

**South** (you)
AK10987

Assume you have NEVER bid this suit and eventually wind up playing in notrump. When you lead the jack from dummy, East plays low. As it is very unlikely that East would not cover holding the queen, play the AK if you need six tricks in the suit.

243. When the number of TRUMP tricks you can afford to lose depends upon whether or not a side suit finesse works, take the side suit finesse BEFORE tackling the trump suit.

**North** (dummy)
♠ AQJ3
♥ 743
♦ A86
♣ KQ4

**South** (you)
♠ 42
♥ AQ10852
♦ K5
♣ AJ10

Your contract is six hearts. The lead is the ♦J. In order to know how to play hearts, you must take the spade finesse first. If the spade finesse loses, you must play hearts for no losers, i.e. lead low to the queen. If the spade finesse wins, make a safety play in hearts by first cashing the ace. If no honor falls, enter dummy and lead a low heart toward your hand.

244. The more desperate the contract, the deeper the finesse you may have to take. It all depends upon the number of tricks you need from the finesse suit.

**North** (dummy)
♠ 1043
♥ KQ103
♦ A32
♣ A32

**South** (you)
♠ AKQJ98
♥ 2
♦ K84
♣ K95

After partner opens the bidding, you cannot restrain yourself and you wind up in six spades. The lead is the ♦J. You have ten tricks on top and can easily develop an eleventh in hearts. But you need TWO extra tricks from the heart suit.

Win the opening lead in your hand, draw trump and lead a heart to the TEN. If West has the ♥J, the slam is yours. Leading a heart to the king will seldom give you two heart tricks no matter who has the ace.

245. Do not squander dummy's treasures just because you have finesseaholic tendencies.

**North** (dummy)
♠ KQJ4
♥ 3
♦ 7654
♣ K543

**South** (you)
♠ 3
♥ AKQ1094
♦ AQ10
♣ A9

You receive the lead of the ♣2 in a contract of six hearts. You win the ♣A, draw trump and lead a spade to the king which holds.

Do not use your two dummy entries to take two diamond finesses although the chance that one of the finesses will succeed is 76%.

100% is better. Lead the queen of spades and discard the ♦10. After this loses, discard the ♦Q on the ♣J.

# CHAPTER 12

# CARD COMBINATIONS & SAFETY PLAYS

Frequently your contract will boil down to the play of ONE suit. Before you attack this one suit, decide how many tricks you need from the suit. The play of the suit may vary depending upon this count. Card combinations are to bridge what verbs are to a language. The sooner you become familiar with the common ones, the faster your game will improve.

The following list of card combinations assumes you are West and the number of tricks you need are in parentheses. Frequently there will be two numbers. This means you may have to play the suit one way for say, four tricks and another for say, five tricks.

When two numbers are given, the smaller number should be taken as the safety play in the suit. Safety plays are taken in wonderful contracts, doubled contracts or anytime that taking the smaller number of tricks is the safest play for the contract. For the sake of simplicity the long suit is in the dummy. Assume you have plenty of entries back and forth.

Tips on how to play these combinations will follow the list. See how well you do before looking at the suggested play. If you have trouble with this sort of exercise (it is most players' bete-noire), you know where you need practice.

|      | West (you) | East (dummy) | Tricks needed. |
|------|-----------|--------------|----------------|
| 246. | Qxx       | J9x          | (1)            |
| 247. | Kxx       | J9x          | (1)            |
| 248. | xxx       | K10x         | (1)            |
| 249. | xxx       | K108         | (1)            |
| 250. | xxx       | K109         | (1)            |
| 251. | xxx       | QJ9          | (1)            |
| 252. | xxx       | Q108         | (1)            |
| 253. | xxx       | AJ9          | (2)            |
| 254. | xxx       | KQ10         | (2)            |
| 255. | Qxx       | A10x         | (2)            |

| 256. | Jxx | A10x | (2) |
|------|------|--------|-----|
| 257. | Jxx | A108 | (2) |
| 258. | Axxx | Q10x | (2) |
| 259. | Kxxx | Q10x | (2) |
| 260. | Qxx | AJ9 | (3) |
| 261. | Jx | AQ9x | (3) |
| 262. | Jx | AK9x | (3) |
| 263. | Jxx | AKxx | (3) |
| 264. | Axx | QJxx | (3) |
| 265. | Ax | J10xxx | (3) |
| 266. | K9x | A10xx | (3) |
| 267. | Q109x | Axxx | (3) |
| 268. | Q1098 | Axxx | (3) |
| 269. | xxx | AKJ10 | (4) |
| 270. | xx | AKJ10 | (4) |
| 271. | xxxx | AJ10xx | (4) |
| 272. | Jxx | AQ10x | (4) |
| 273. | KQx | A10xx | (4) |
| 274. | K9 | A10xxx | (4) |
| 275. | A9 | KJxxx | (4) |
| 276. | Ax | K109xx | (4) |
| 277. | Axxx | KJ10x | (4) |
| 278. | x | AQ109xx | (5) |
| 279. | xx | AKJ10x | (5) |
| 280. | xxx | AKJ10x | (5) |
| 281. | Jx | AQxxxx | (5) |
| 282. | Jx | AQ76xx | (5) |

| | | | |
|---|---|---|---|
| 283. | A | J10xxxx | (4) |
| 284. | A10xx | Jxxx | (2) (3) |
| 285. | 10xx | KQxx | (2) (3) |
| 286. | Axx | KJxx | (3) (4) |
| 287. | xx | AKQ10x | (4) (5) |
| 288. | A9x | KJxxx | (4) (5) |
| 289. | J10x | AK8xx | (4) (5) |
| 290. | x | AJ10xxx | (4) (5) |
| 291. | x | AKQ10xx | (5) (6) |
| 292. | Jx | AK98xx | (5) (6) |
| 293. | xx | AK109xx | (5) (6) |
| 294. | xxx | AQ10xxx | (5) (6) |
| 295. | x | KQxxxxx | (5) (6) |

## THE WINNING TIPS

246. Low to the queen and low to the nine.

247. Low to the king and low to the nine. However if LHO is MARKED with the AQ, play low to the jack the second time.

248. Low to the ten and low to the king.

249. Low to the eight. If the eight drives out the jack or queen, lead low to the ten. If the eight loses to the nine, lead low to the king.

250. Low to the nine and low to the ten. However, if the ace is MARKED to your left, lead low to the king the second time.

251. Low to the jack and low to the queen. However if RHO is marked with both the ace and the king, lead low to the jack and then low to the nine.

252. Low to the ten and low to the queen. However if the AK is MARKED to your right, lead low to the eight originally.

253. Low to the nine and if it loses to an honor, lead low to the jack. If LHO plays an honor the first time you lead the suit, win the ace, return to your hand and lead low to the nine.

254. Low to the king and if it loses, low to the ten. If the king holds, lead low a second time from your hand and if West plays low, hope you can guess the position. However, if LHO is incapable of ducking TWICE, play the ten the second time. On the other hand, if RHO is incapable of ducking once, play the queen.

255. Low to the queen and if it loses, low to the ten.

256. Low to the ten and then the ace.

257. Run the jack. If it loses, lead low to the ten. If the jack is covered, win the ace, return to your hand and lead low to the eight.

258. Low to the ten. If it loses to the jack, lead low to the queen.

259. Low to the king and if it wins or loses, low to the ten.

260. Play the queen. If it is covered, return to your hand and play low to the nine. However if you KNOW LHO has a singleton or a doubleton, lead low to the jack originally.

261. Low to the jack and whether it wins or loses, low to the nine next.

262. Low to the jack. If it loses, low to the nine.

263. Ace and low to the jack.

264. Ace and low to the jack. If the jack wins, return to your hand and lead low to the queen. Next best is leading low to the jack originally.

265. Ace and then low from both hands. You are hoping for honor doubleton. If the suit is 3-3, you always make three tricks.

266. Low to the nine and then the king and ace.

267. Ace and low to the ten.

268. Run the ten. If it loses to the jack, run the queen.

269. Ace and then low to the ten.

270. Low to the ten. You may need to take TWO finesses.

271. Low to the ten and if it loses, low to the jack. However if you have reason to believe that RHO has an honor, begin by playing low to the ace.

272. Low to the ten and if it wins, low to the queen. Do not squander the jack. LHO may have a doubleton king. Play the same with Qxx facing AJ10x.

273. King, queen and low to the ace.

274. Low to the nine and then the king and ace.

275. Low to the nine and then the king and ace.

276. Ace and low to the king. RHO is more likely to have honor doubleton than two small.

277. Ace and low to the ten. Better than the king and running the jack. Playing the ace first allows you to pick up the suit if LHO has four cards.

278. Low to the queen in case RHO has Jx.

279. Low to the ten and if it wins, low to the jack.

280. Ace and then low to the ten. As long as you can still take TWO finesses, you can afford to cash one high honor first.

281. Play the ace in case 4th hand has a singleton king, the only 4-1 distribution that matters.

282. Run the jack. If it is covered win the ace and if RHO plays the eight, nine or ten, return to your hand and lead low to the six.

283. Play the ace (nice play), enter dummy and then lead LOW. You must find the suit 3-3 or one hand with a doubleton honor. Play the same if dummy has J108xxx.

284. For two tricks, lead the ace and low to the jack. For three tricks, lead low to the ten and then the ace.

285. For two tricks, lead low to the queen and then low to the ten. For three tricks, lead low to the queen. If it holds return to your hand and lead low to the king. You must find LHO with Ace third or AJ doubleton.

286. For three tricks, play the king, the ace and then low to the jack. For four tricks, play the ace and low to the jack or low to the jack.

287. For four tricks, play the ace and then low to the ten. (With no side dummy entry, play low to the ten originally). For five tricks, play the AKQ.

288. For four tricks, play the king and low to the nine. If RHO shows out on the second play, win the ace and lead low to the jack. For five tricks, play low to the jack.

289. For four tricks, lead low to the ten in case either player has the missing five cards. For five tricks, run the jack. If it holds, continue with the ten in case LHO has Q9xx.

290. For four tricks, lead the ace and then a low card. For five tricks, lead low to the jack.

291. For five tricks, lead low to the ten. For six tricks, lead the AKQ.

292. For five tricks, cash the ace and then run the jack. For six tricks, run the jack. If it is covered, win and later lead low to the eight.

293. For five tricks, play the ace and then lead low to the nine. For six tricks, lead low to the nine.

294. For five tricks, cash the ace. If no honor falls, return to your hand and then lead toward dummy. For six tricks, lead low to the queen.

295. For five tricks, play low from both hands in case RHO has a singleton ace. If the suit breaks 3-2, you always have five tricks.

   For six tricks, lead low to the queen. You must hope LHO has Ax.

# CHAPTER 13

# DISCARDS

Isn't it the defenders who usually have to make discards? Yes, but who has to watch these discards? You do, the declarer. In addition, you must plan discards when you are running a long suit or worse, plan discards when they are running a long suit.

296. Opponents are never too thrilled to make EARLY discards BEFORE they have an idea of the make-up of your hand. Early discards frequently translate into extra tricks for you.

297. Know your opponents' discarding methods. Do they play (1) STANDARD (high encouraging, low discouraging); (2) UPSIDE DOWN (high discouraging, low encouraging); (3) ODD-EVEN (odd encouraging, even discouraging) etc.?

298. Most players generally discard from length rather than shortness. Discards from five and six card suits emerge much more quickly than discards from three or four card suits.

299. It is easier to discard from a suit headed by the ace than a suit headed by the queen. If an opponent has no trouble making discards in a suit in which you are missing both the ace and the queen, he is more likely to have the ace than the queen.

300. Along the same vein, it is easier to discard from a suit headed by the king than from one headed by the jack or queen. A word to the wise.

301. Before running a long suit, be sure you have enough safe discards to make. If you haven't, develop the necessary number of outside tricks BEFORE running the long suit.

**North** (dummy)
♠ 53
♥ 87
♦ AKQJ876
♣ 54

**South** (you)
♠ KQ10
♥ QJ32
♦ 1042
♣ KQ3

You arrive at 3NT and West leads a low spade to the jack and king. Although it is tempting to run the diamonds, it is self-destructive. You will have to make FOUR discards from your hand. What will they be? You can afford to discard one club and one heart but what will you discard on the sixth diamond—let alone the seventh? It won't be pretty. Better to establish a ninth trick in either black suit BEFORE running the diamonds.

302. The discard of a high honor generally shows the HIGHEST of a sequence of honors. It denies a higher equal honor. Thus the discard of a king shows KQJ10 and denies the ace. The discard of a queen shows QJ109(x) and denies the king. The discard of an ace tells partner that he has led the wrong suit.

303. If necessary, experienced players will routinely bare down to singleton queens or kings on the run of a long suit. Weaker players are loathe to do the same.

304. Experienced players seldom, if ever, suffer over discards. It gives away too much information. Suffering defenders usually have been forced to make painful discards. See previous tip.

305. If you are running a long suit and have to make several discards, it is a good idea to make your first discard in a suit you wish to encourage the opponents to discard. Opponents tend to discard the same suit that you are discarding.

306. At times a contract will seem hopeless because you have to knock out an ace, and you know that the player with that ace has the setting tricks in another suit. All may not be lost. If that player is also guarding a third suit, pressure from a few discards may do him in.

**North** (dummy)
♠ K43
♥ 75
♦ AJ92
♣ QJ109

**West**
♠ 9876
♥ 963
♦ 43
♣ 8632

**East**
♠ QJ2
♥ KQJ42
♦ 105
♣ A75

**South** (you)
♠ A105
♥ A108
♦ KQ876
♣ K4

Playing 5 card majors, East opens one heart. You overcall 1NT and partner raises to 3NT. West leads a low heart and you win the third round of the suit. With eight sure tricks you would like to establish your ninth in clubs. The rub is that you know East has the ace of clubs along with the setting trick in hearts. What to do?

Run the diamonds forcing three discards from East. It is easy for East to part with two clubs but the third discard squeezes East in three suits! If East parts with a spade, you make an extra trick in that suit. If East discards a heart winner, you can establish your ninth trick in clubs.

307. If you are planning on running dummy's long suit and must make several discards, plan them in ADVANCE. Avoid making painful discards. It gives away too much information.

308. A defender who discards established winners at notrump presumably has no outside entry (or he is being squeezed out of his winners). If you are missing an ace, presumably it is in the other defender's hand.

309. If the previous play has marked you with a particular card or cards and you have a chance to make several discards, try to discard the cards you are known to hold. If you keep these cards, you will not be able to fool your opponents in the end game.

**North** (dummy)
43

**West**
K765

**East**
Q982

**South** (you)
AJ10

West leads low to East's queen and your ace. At this point West knows that you have the jack. Later in the hand, if you have all the tricks but one and are discarding losers from your hand, discard the jack, the card you are known to hold. Discarding the ten instead of the jack sends you tumbling back to preschool.

310. When you have a weak suit that you wish to conceal and must give up the lead early in a side suit, do not draw trump first. You may give an opponent a chance to make a revealing discard.

**North** (dummy)
♠ KQ1092
♥ 942
♦ 43
♣ 853

**West**
♠ 74
♥ A75
♦ K1096
♣ Q942

**East**
♠ 3
♥ KQJ10
♦ 8752
♣ J1076

**South** (you)
♠ AJ865
♥ 863
♦ AQJ
♣ AK

After you receive a single raise in spades you leap to game. West, with honors in every suit, elects to lead a trump.

Win the lead in dummy and take the diamond finesse immediately. Do not draw the last trump first. You do not want to give East a chance to signal in hearts. Upon winning the ♦K, West must guess what to do. Had you drawn a second trump, East would discard the ♥K. West would no longer have to guess what to do.

311. When cashing winners in an equally divided suit, force the player you think will have discarding problems to make as many discards as possible before seeing any discards from his partner.

**North** (dummy)
AQ103

**West**
76

**East**
942

**South** (you)
KJ85

Say you think that West has the most of the enemy strength and could be helped by seeing a discard from East. Play the fourth round of the suit from YOUR hand forcing West to make two discards before he can see even one discard from East.

If East were the player with the stronger hand, play the fourth round of the suit from DUMMY forcing East to discard before he can see his partner's second discard.

312.   Sometimes a discard can be used to unblock a suit.

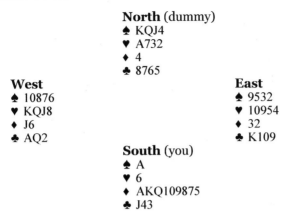

**North** (dummy)
♠ KQJ4
♥ A732
♦ 4
♣ 8765

**West**
♠ 10876
♥ KQJ8
♦ J6
♣ AQ2

**East**
♠ 9532
♥ 10954
♦ 32
♣ K109

**South** (you)
♠ A
♥ 6
♦ AKQ109875
♣ J43

After West opens one club and East passes, you wind up in five diamonds (bring back 3NT). West leads the king of hearts. Your best (only) chance is to duck and hope a heart is continued. If it is, you can win the ace of hearts and make the spectacular unblock of the ace of spades. This liberates the ♠KQJ upon which you can discard three clubs and make six. At this point most partners will ask why you didn't bid six.

313.   And now for a tip you cannot use. When you wish to force the opponents to make innumerable discards, revoke! (Just kidding).

**North** (dummy)
♠ Q32
♥ J4
♦ AKQ82
♣ Q32

**South** (you)
♠ A7
♥ 1087
♦ J10763
♣ KJ5

You arrive at 3NT and West leads a low spade. You try the queen but East covers. How do you like your chances? Here's how the late great Harold Harkavy played the hand. He took the first trick, crossed to the ♦A—all following—and played the king, queen and eight of diamonds, DISCARDING HEARTS! He then led dummy's remaining diamond, the deuce, over to his FOUR remaining diamonds scoring a total of eight diamond tricks. East, with a singleton diamond, had to make seven discards without noticing the revokes while West, with a doubleton diamond, only had to make six!

314. Some opponents give count with their first discard; others give attitude. Still others, when making two discards in the same suit give attitude on the first discard and present count on the second. The point is to know what discarding agreements the opponents have.

315. The three most common discarding methods are: "Standard" = low discouraging, high encouraging; "Upside down" = low encouraging, high discouraging; "Odd-Even" = odd encouraging, even discouraging.

In addition, the discard of an even card is considered a suit preference play. A low even discard indicates strength in the lower ranking side suit; a high even discard indicates strength in the higher ranking side suit.

316. A player who makes a discard in your second bid suit will generally have three, or more likely five, cards in the suit. Not four.

# CHAPTER 14

# ENTRIES

Virtually every hand you play deals with entries. Virtually every plan made must take entries into account. There are many ways to create entries, some quite daring. The bottom line is to know how many entries you need and, equally important, how to secure them.

317.  Once you decide which suit you are planning to establish, keep as many entries to that hand as possible.

318.  As a general rule, try to retain entries to the weaker of the two hands.

319.  Ducking tricks in long suits is a common entry-saving technique.

**North** (dummy)
AK432

**South** (you)
765

At notrump with no side dummy entries, duck once to try for four tricks. If you only need three, duck twice. If this is a side suit at a trump contract play the same, only draw trump first.

320.  At times you must duck a round of a suit before taking a finesse.

**North** (dummy)
AQ432

**South** (you)
65

For four tricks lead low from dummy (in case East, holding the king, is the nervous type), and then lead low to the queen hoping to find West with Kxx.

321.  Unblocking from honor doubleton when dummy has NO OUTSIDE ENTRY can be a neat way of creating an entry, a finesse position, and a trick.

**North** (dummy)
Q109

**West**
J872

**East**
A654

**South** (you)
K3

West leads low and East plays the ace. With no side dummy entry, unblock the king and later lead low to the ten. (West is marked with the jack from East's play of the ace).

322.

**North** (dummy)
A1043

**West**
J872

**East**
K95

**South** (you)
Q6

West leads low, dummy plays low and East plays the king. Unblock the queen and later lead low to the ten. Play the same with Jx. (These second round finesses presume you need two tricks in the suit).

323. With three cards in your hand including a high middle spot card opposite four or more cards in the dummy—one of which is the LOWER EQUAL of your middle card—begin by leading the middle card from the three card holding. Would somebody please repeat that in English?

**North** (dummy)
KQ92

**West**
J8764

**East**
3

**South** (you)
A105

Assume an entryless dummy and you need four tricks in the suit. Begin by leading the TEN to the king, then low to your ace. You retain the option of either leading low to the queen or low to the nine. If you fail to unblock the ten, you will not be able to take four tricks in the suit even though you know West has the jack.

324. A similar example, this time the jack is the middle card.

**North** (dummy)
K1082

**West**
Q976

**East**
54

**South** (you)
AJ3

You need four tricks and dummy has no side entry. Begin with the jack. Assume West covers. Win the king, and return to the ace. You now have the OPTION of leading low to the ten or low to the eight. A great player like you will get a count and then make the winning play.

325. Although most early unblocking plays begin by leading the ten or the jack, don't overlook those precious middle eights and nines.

**North** (dummy)
KJ86

**West**　　　　　　　　　　　　　　　　　　**East**
10752　　　　　　　　　　　　　　　　　　　A3

**South** (you)
Q94

Hoping for three tricks, lead the NINE to the jack. If East wins, later play the queen leaving yourself the OPTION of leading low to the eight or low to the king.

Let's backtrack. Assume when you lead the nine to the jack, East ducks. When you lead low to the queen, East plays the ace. Be prepared to unblock the queen, leaving a later option.

326.　　　　　　　　　　　**North** (dummy)
　　　　　　　　　　　　　　K1074

**West**　　　　　　　　　　　　　　　　　　**East**
Q532　　　　　　　　　　　　　　　　　　　J9

**South** (you)
A86

You need three tricks and there are no side dummy entries. Lead the EIGHT to the ten. (Or the ace and then the eight to the ten). Later cash the ace leaving yourself the option of leading low to the king or low to the seven!

327. If the three card holding is in the dummy and the length in your hand, begin by leading the blocking middle card from dummy.

**North** (dummy)
K106

**West**　　　　　　　　　　　　　　　　　　**East**
J7　　　　　　　　　　　　　　　　　　　　Q854

**South** (you)
A932

You need three tricks and you have no outside entry to your hand. Lead the ten and let it go whether or not it is covered. Later lead the king and then decide whether to lead low to the ace or low to the nine.

328. When a suit has all the earmarks of being blocked (the higher spot cards in the shorter hand), look for a chance to discard one of those spot cards.

**North** (dummy)
K5432

**West**　　　　　　　　　　　　　　　　　　**East**
6　　　　　　　　　　　　　　　　　　　　J87

**South** (you)
AQ109

You need five tricks and there is no side entry to dummy. All you can do is play the ace and the queen and hope the jack drops. If it doesn't, the suit is blocked. However if you can DISCARD the nine or ten from your hand, perhaps on one of THEIR winners, five tricks are yours.

329. A common entry-saving technique is to duck one round of a suit when holding Axxxx(x) facing a small doubleton. This ducking play saves one entry and can be used effectively at either suit or notrump contracts.

330. In order to create an extra dummy entry, you might have to win a trick with a higher card than necessary.

**North** (dummy)
KJ4

**West**　　　　　　　　　　　　　　　　　　**East**
Q9873　　　　　　　　　　　　　　　　　　62

**South** (you)
A105

West leads the seven and you can win the ten. However if you need two dummy entries, win with the ace and later finesse the jack.

331.

**North** (dummy)
QJ4

**West**　　　　　　　　　　　　　　　　　　**East**
K8732　　　　　　　　　　　　　　　　　　95

**South** (you)
A106

West leads low and you need a LATER dummy entry. Win the first trick with the ACE. Greedy players have a hard time with this. They invariably win a trick as cheaply as possible. Later when they desperately need to get to dummy, they can't.

332.

**North** (dummy)
J32

**West**　　　　　　　　　　　　　　　　　　**East**
Q9874　　　　　　　　　　　　　　　　　　6

**South** (you)
AK105

West leads the seven and you can win the trick with the ten (or the jack) if you like. However if you need a LATER entry to entry to dummy, take the trick with the king or ace.

333. You must be prepared to take seemingly unnecessary finesses if you need extra entries to one hand or the other.

**North** (dummy)
AQ10

**South** (you)
K43

If you need THREE dummy entries, lead the king to the ace and later low to the ten.

334. At times you must play for a defensive error when looking for an extra entry.

**North** (dummy)
AJ3

**South** (you)
K4 or Q4

If you need two dummy entries, lead low to the jack and hope second hand doesn't play high.

335. Another entry saving technique is to overtake a winner if the spot cards and the number of tricks needed warrant the play.

**North** (dummy)
K9872

**West**
J543

**East**
106

**South** (you)
AQ

If you need exactly FOUR tricks from this suit and there is ONE side entry to dummy, play the ace and overtake the queen. If the suit breaks 3-3, or the

ten or jack drops doubleton, you have four tricks. If you don't overtake, a 3-3 break is your only hope for four tricks.

336. Leading the nine from J9x or Q9x when partner has AQ10x, AQ10xx, AJ10x or AJ10xx is an entry-saving technique.

**North** (dummy)
AJ102

**West**
K876

**East**
54

**South** (you)
Q93

Lead the nine and underplay the deuce. Continue with the queen. You wind up with four tricks never having to return to your hand to repeat the finesse. If you begin with the queen and West does not cover, you will need a return hand entry to secure four tricks against best defense.

337. If you need an entry badly enough and you can afford to lose a trick to get it, you may have to make a really desperate play.

**North** (dummy)
92

**West**
1087

**East**
65

**South** (you)
AKQJ43

If you absolutely must get to dummy, lead low to the nine and hope West has the ten. If it all works out, you may see your name in a newspaper column.

338. If your only hand entries are in the trump suit, you may have to defer drawing trumps.

**North** (dummy)
♠ KQ54
♥ 3
♦ 98764
♣ A32

**South** (you)
♠ 32
♥ AKQJ109
♦ J2
♣ K54

You wind up in four hearts and West leads the ♣Q. In order to make this hand, West must have the ♠A in which case you can park a club on a spade. Even if West has the needed ♠A, you may have to lead spades TWICE from your hand. Win the opening lead in your hand conserving the ♣A for a later entry.

At trick two lead a spade. Do not even think of drawing trump first. You need to return to your hand with a trump if West ducks the first spade. Assume he does. Now draw trump and lead a second spade. If West has the ♠A the hand is over. If East has the ♠A the hand is also over...for you.

339. Ruffing low with a powerful trump suit can usually be classified as a careless error. The low trump might serve as a possible dummy entry.

**North** (dummy)
543

**West**
98

**East**
76

**South** (you)
AKQJ102

If forced to ruff, ruff high. If trumps divide 2-2, you have a later dummy entry.

340. A careful declarer draws trumps with an eye to entries and flexibility.

**North** (dummy)
K532

**West**
876

**East**
9

**South** (you)
AQJ104

Begin by playing the queen and the jack. If it becomes necessary to draw a third round of trump, lead the TEN. This leaves you with a later trump entry to either hand regardless of where you win the trick.

341. Before drawing trump, decide where you want to end up. Don't surprise yourself.

342. "Eight ever, nine never" is only a nursery rhyme when entry considerations enter the picture.

**North** (dummy)
♠ 943
♥ A72
♦ 732
♣ K876

**South** (you)
♠ AKJ1076
♥ 654
♦ AK4
♣ A

Against silent opposition you get to four spades. West makes the seemingly killing lead of the ♥K. As this lead removes your only certain entry to the ♣K, you stand to lose four tricks; two hearts, one diamond and possibly one spade. Not to worry. Win the ♥A and lead a spade to the JACK. If this finesse wins you have 10 tricks; if it loses, the nine of spades becomes the entry to the ♣K (after you unblock the ace).

If either defender shows out on the first spade and ♠J wins the trick, cash the ace of clubs and lead the ♠10. The defender with the ♠Q must either win the trick and give you a dummy entry or lose his trump trick.

343. Can't get to dummy? A trump loser, natural or created, may be the answer.

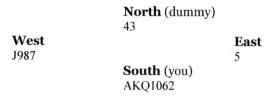

**North** (dummy)
43

**West**
J987

**East**
5

**South** (you)
AKQ1062

Assume this is your trump suit. You play the AKQ and West remains with the master trump. Perhaps at the proper moment you can exit a trump and force West to give you a dummy entry. Here is an even more advanced application of this principle.

**North** (dummy)

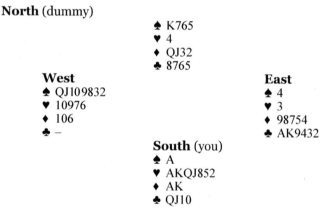

                   ♠ K765
                   ♥ 4
                   ♦ QJ32
                   ♣ 8765

**West**
♠ QJ109832
♥ 10976
♦ 106
♣ –

**East**
♠ 4
♥ 3
♦ 98754
♣ AK9432

**South** (you)
♠ A
♥ AKQJ852
♦ AK
♣ QJ10

West opens three spades passed around to you and you take a flyer by bidding six hearts.

West leads the ♠Q and things look bleak. You win the opening lead and play two top hearts. East discards a humongous club on the second heart. Any chance? Of course. Why else would this hand be in here? West is marked with 11 major suit cards. Maybe the other two are diamonds. Cash the ♥Q, the ♦AK and exit with the ♥2. West must win and play a spade. Miracle of miracles, you can discard all of your clubs on the king of spades and the winning diamonds.

344. It pays to recognize common card combinations when entry problems may exist.

**North** (dummy)
AJ102

**West**                                                     **East**
K765                                                     Q4

**South** (you)
983

Assume you need three tricks from this suit. The lead is in your hand, dummy has side entries but you have only ONE entry back to your hand. Lead the THREE to the ten. Later return to your hand and run the nine. If you lead the nine first, you will need TWO reentries to your hand to pick up the suit.

345.  Even the simplest of positions can lead to disaster if you do not cater to your entry problems.

**North** (dummy)
J104

**West**                                                     **East**
AK76                                                    982

**South** (you)
Q53

Suit or notrump, if West leads high and you need a dummy entry, play the queen.

346.  With no clear cut need of extra entries to either hand, maintain entry flexibility.

**North** (dummy)
AQ4

**South** (you)
K76

If this suit is led, it is usually best to take the trick in dummy with the queen retaining later entry flexibility to either hand. It is also more deceptive than winning with either the ace or the king.

347.  At times you must restrain yourself from making seemingly routine plays when an entry problem exists.

**North** (dummy)
A76

**West**                                                     **East**
103                                                     KJ984

**South** (you)
Q52

You are playing a notrump contract after East has bid spades. West leads the ♠10. Ninety-nine times out of 100 you would play low from dummy to ensure two tricks. However if you need a LATER entry to your hand, win the ace. If you play low and East does not take the king, you will be forced to win the queen prematurely.

348. When entries to the weaker hand are at a premium, TLC with what you have may be necessary.

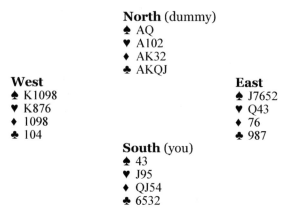

**North** (dummy)
♠ AQ
♥ A102
♦ AK32
♣ AKQJ

**West**
♠ K1098
♥ K876
♦ 1098
♣ 104

**East**
♠ J7652
♥ Q43
♦ 76
♣ 987

**South** (you)
♠ 43
♥ J95
♦ QJ54
♣ 6532

Because of system you wind up playing six diamonds. The lead is the ♦ 10. WHEN THINGS LOOK BLEAK, THINK POSITIVELY. You must find split honors in hearts plus the ♠K with West. Do you have the entries? YES! Draw trump ending in your hand and lead the FIVE of hearts to the ten. East wins and exits a club. Return to your hand with a trump and play the JACK of hearts. Whether West covers or not, you can still arrange to take the spade finesse. If you play hearts in any other order, down you go.

If your hearts were 109x facing AJx or 109x facing AQx, your play is to lead a low heart to the jack or queen. Later run the ten. Assuming the heart honors are divided, you will have an entry to take the spade finesse.

349. When you can win a trick in either hand, do not make a play until you have a plan. Reread this one.

**North** (dummy)
♠ AJ842
♥ A103
♦ Q4
♣ J76

**South** (you)
♠ 53
♥ K5
♦ KJ1092
♣ 10854

You wind up in 1NT and West leads the ♥Q. Looking only at hearts, you should win the king so you can later finesse the ten. But looking at the whole hand, it is more important to keep the ♥K as a later hand entry to the diamonds. Play the ♥A and follow with the ♦Q to make sure of seven tricks.

350. A nifty unblock may be necessary to conserve an entry.

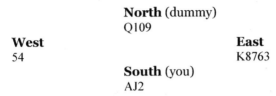

**North** (dummy)
Q109

**West**
54

**East**
K8763

**South** (you)
AJ2

With the lead in dummy and a shortage of dummy entries, lead the queen. If it is not covered, underplay the jack. Assuming the queen holds, run the ten. Whether East covers or not, you can still arrange to lead another suit from the dummy.

351. The stronger the trump suit, the more careful you must be to conserve trump entries to the hand that you are establishing.

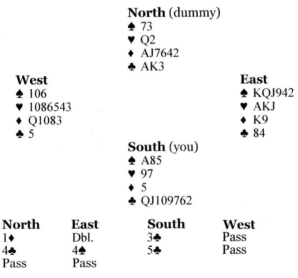

**North** (dummy)
♠ 73
♥ Q2
♦ AJ7642
♣ AK3

**West**
♠ 106
♥ 1086543
♦ Q1083
♣ 5

**East**
♠ KQJ942
♥ AKJ
♦ K9
♣ 84

**South** (you)
♠ A85
♥ 97
♦ 5
♣ QJ109762

| North | East | South | West |
|-------|------|-------|------|
| 1♦ | Dbl. | 3♣ | Pass |
| 4♣ | 4♠ | 5♣ | Pass |
| Pass | Pass | | |

Opening lead: ♠10

The only hope is to set up the diamonds. Assuming a normal 4-2 division, THREE diamonds must be ruffed. This requires three dummy entries outside of the ♦A. If that ♣3 doesn't look like an entry to you, get a new pair of glasses. If you ruff diamonds HIGH, conserving your beloved DEUCE, you will be able to set up the diamonds eventually leading the ♣2 to dummy's three. Your partner will love you and the ♣2 will be proud of you.

352. When the opponents lead a suit in which you have a blocking middle card, unblock that middle card.

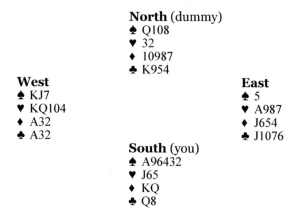

**North** (dummy)
♠ Q108
♥ 32
♦ 10987
♣ K954

**West**
♠ KJ7
♥ KQ104
♦ A32
♣ A32

**East**
♠ 5
♥ A987
♦ J654
♣ J1076

**South** (you)
♠ A96432
♥ J65
♦ KQ
♣ Q8

West opens 1NT and you buy the hand at two spades. West leads the king and a low heart to East's ace. East shifts to a trump.

You duck, West wins, and returns a low trump which you would like to be able to win in your hand in order to ruff your last heart. If you take the precaution of unblocking the ♠10 at trick three, it is easy to win the trump return in your hand with the nine and ruff a heart. However if you neglect to unblock the ♠10, you pay. You cannot get back to your hand to ruff your third heart without giving West a chance to play a third trump.

353. Optimism plus a plan may be the recipe to overcome a shortage of entries.

**North** (dummy)
♠ K73
♥ AK762
♦ 982
♣ 108

**West**
♠ 1096
♥ 1098
♦ A53
♣ KQJ9

**East**
♠ 42
♥ Q5
♦ KQ74
♣ 65432

**South** (you)
♠ AQJ85
♥ J43
♦ J106
♣ A7

You get to a pushy four spade contract and West leads the ♣K. Things are so bad that you need the ♥Q to drop PLUS the player with the queen to have only two spades. Go for it. Win the ♣A, play two high trump honors from your hand and then the ♥AK. When the ♥Q drops, cash the ♥J and enter dummy with a trump and discard two minor suit losers on the hearts. You have just made an overtrick. Good players are also lucky players.

354. Discarding a high blocking honor(s) is one way of liberating a blocked suit.

**North** (dummy)
♠ 43
♥ K10965
♦ KQJ10
♣ AK

**South** (you)
♠ AKQJ1098
♥ 7432
♦ A
♣ 2

East doubles your six spade contract asking for a heart lead, dummy's first bid suit. Alas, West is void in hearts and leads the ♣Q. Win the ♣AK and jettison your ♦A. Now discard as many heart losers as you can on dummy's diamonds.

355. No matter how strong a suit is, you may have to take a finesse in that suit in order to create an extra entry. Imagination! Courage! Luck!

**North** (dummy)
♠ J643
♥ 97
♦ 9842
♣ Q87

**South** (you)
♠ AQ
♥ AKQJ1054
♦ K3
♣ 95

After East opens one club you become declarer in four hearts. West leads the king and a club and East continues a third club which you ruff HIGH, West discarding a low diamond. You need two dummy entries, one to finesse the spade, one to lead up to the ♦K. In order to create two entries, lead a heart to the seven! Does it work? What difference? It is the right play.

356. There is no greater sacrifice than a possible trick for a sure entry. Of course the entry must be worth more than the trick you are sacrificing.

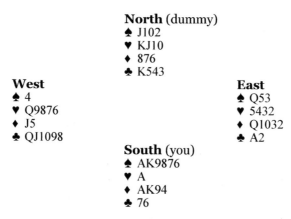

**North** (dummy)
- ♠ J102
- ♥ KJ10
- ♦ 876
- ♣ K543

**West**
- ♠ 4
- ♥ Q9876
- ♦ J5
- ♣ QJ1098

**East**
- ♠ Q53
- ♥ 5432
- ♦ Q1032
- ♣ A2

**South** (you)
- ♠ AK9876
- ♥ A
- ♦ AK94
- ♣ 76

Your contract is four spades and West leads the ♣Q which holds. East wins the second club play (you duck again) and shifts to a low diamond. In order to lock up this contract, cash your major suit aces and exit with a low spade. The dummy has a forced trump entry and you can eventually dispose of both diamonds on royalty.

357. A finesse is a finesse is a finesse, but not when there is a shortage of entries.

**North** (dummy)
- ♠ AK
- ♥ 87652
- ♦ 764
- ♣ QJ10

**South** (you)
- ♠ QJ10986
- ♥ AJ
- ♦ A52
- ♣ A4

You get to four spades and West leads a trump. With three red suit losers staring you in the face, you must work with those clubs. Don't finesse! If the finesse loses and a trump is returned, the clubs are blocked with no way to untangle them. Simply play the ace and a club establishing your tenth trick in clubs with the ♠K as your entry.

358. Once you decide to set up a long suit, you can never protect too many entries to that hand.

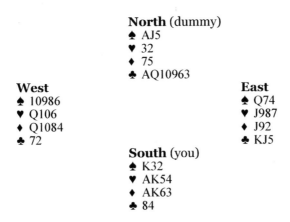

**North** (dummy)
♠ AJ5
♥ 32
♦ 75
♣ AQ10963

**West**
♠ 10986
♥ Q106
♦ Q1084
♣ 72

**East**
♠ Q74
♥ J987
♦ J92
♣ KJ5

**South** (you)
♠ K32
♥ AK54
♦ AK63
♣ 84

You wind up in 3NT and West leads the ♠10. You must work with clubs, so save as many dummy entries as possible. In other words, do not play the ♠J at trick one. Win the ♠K and lead a club to the queen and king. East wins, but cannot attack dummy's spade entry. Once East returns a red suit, you have time to set up the club suit. If you play the ♠J at trick one (not looking ahead), you pay dearly. After winning the ♣K, East can safely return a spade knocking out dummy's remaining entry. When the clubs do not come home, it is too sad for words.

359. When planning to ruff losers in dummy, ask yourself how many hand entries you need and make appropriate provisions.

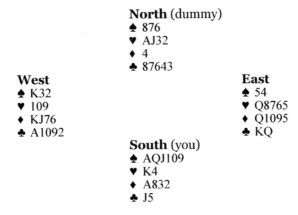

**North** (dummy)
♠ 876
♥ AJ32
♦ 4
♣ 87643

**West**
♠ K32
♥ 109
♦ KJ76
♣ A1092

**East**
♠ 54
♥ Q8765
♦ Q1095
♣ KQ

**South** (you)
♠ AQJ109
♥ K4
♦ A832
♣ J5

You wander into four spades and West leads the ♥10. Your plan should be to try to ruff three diamonds in dummy, eventually conceding two clubs and a spade. Win the opening lead in DUMMY, play the ace and ruff a diamond; return to the king of hearts and ruff another diamond. Now for the key play. Ruff the ♥J with the ♠A and ruff your fourth diamond in dummy. You lose two clubs and one spade. Win the opening lead in your hand and you can kiss another game contract adios.

As a secondary tip, notice your trump spots when planning to do some ruffing. If you have them all, as you do in this diagram, you may have to ruff a loser with a high trump to avoid an embarrassing overruff followed by an even more embarrassing trump return.

360. It is not always right to draw trumps once a long suit is established. The correct play may depend upon the number of trump tricks you can afford to lose.

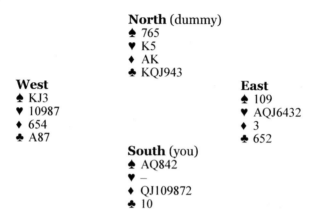

**North** (dummy)
- ♠ 765
- ♥ K5
- ♦ AK
- ♣ KQJ943

**West**
- ♠ KJ3
- ♥ 10987
- ♦ 654
- ♣ A87

**East**
- ♠ 109
- ♥ AQJ6432
- ♦ 3
- ♣ 652

**South** (you)
- ♠ AQ842
- ♥ —
- ♦ QJ109872
- ♣ 10

After East preempts in hearts you wind up in five diamonds. You ruff the opening heart lead and lead a club to West's ace. West forces your hand with a second heart play. When you enter dummy with the ♦K both follow, leaving two trumps at large. As you can afford to lose one more trick, do not play the second high trump from dummy. Play winning clubs. After West ruffs, win any return, draw the last trump ending in dummy and discard your remaining spades on winning clubs.

361. At notrump it is frequently right to run a long suit and force discards. However if the long suit is needed for communications, don't run it.

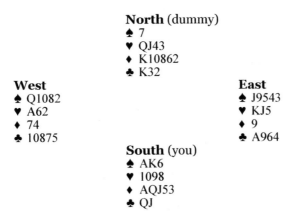

**North** (dummy)
♠ 7
♥ QJ43
♦ K10862
♣ K32

**West**
♠ Q1082
♥ A62
♦ 74
♣ 10875

**East**
♠ J9543
♥ KJ5
♦ 9
♣ A964

**South** (you)
♠ AK6
♥ 1098
♦ AQJ53
♣ QJ

You play 3NT and West leads the ♠2. You have seven tricks on the go and do not have time to fool with the hearts. Your play is to set up two tricks in clubs. If you run diamonds first and then drive out the ♣A, how are you going to untangle the clubs if East wins the first club and returns a spade? Answer: You are not. Solution: leave at least one diamond entry in dummy before attacking clubs.

362. When all else fails, the opponents may be right there to help you out.

**North** (dummy)
♠ 76
♥ 742
♦ 5432
♣ QJ106

**West**
♠ J1098
♥ 863
♦ J987
♣ 53

**East**
♠ 542
♥ 1095
♦ 106
♣ A8742

**South** (you)
♠ AKQ3
♥ AKQJ
♦ AKQ
♣ K9

Do you like your hand? You open 5NT. Partner, afraid to pass, bids 6NT. West leads the ♠J. You are faced with both a club and a spade loser. When things look dark project a winning scenario (wishful thinking). Perhaps someone holds the singleton ace of clubs. Perhaps one of your opponents will take the first club. Perhaps there will be no more taxes. Perhaps the player with the ♣A will only have clubs when you finally lead your second club.

Win the spade and play the ♣K which holds. Continue by cashing all of your remaining winners reducing to a club and a spade. Dummy remains with two clubs. Exit with a club. If the player with the ♣A has nothing left but clubs, he must put you back in dummy. How sweet it is.

363. At notrump, if dummy has either KQJxx or AQJxx facing xx in your hand and there is only one side entry, you may need to make a safety play. If you need exactly THREE tricks start by playing LOW from BOTH hands. If you lead low to an honor originally, you expose yourself to a defensive holdup play.

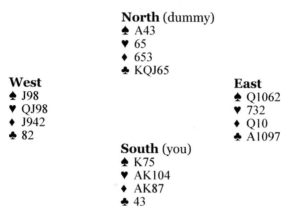

**North** (dummy)
♠ A43
♥ 65
♦ 653
♣ KQJ65

**West**
♠ J98
♥ QJ98
♦ J942
♣ 82

**East**
♠ Q1062
♥ 732
♦ Q10
♣ A1097

**South** (you)
♠ K75
♥ AK104
♦ AK87
♣ 43

You open 1NT and partner raises to game. West leads the ♥Q. With six top tricks and no suit the opponents can quickly establish that your goal is to secure THREE club tricks.

Duck a club at trick two. East wins and returns a heart which you win. Now drive out the ♣A. East wins and returns his last heart. The opponents score two hearts and two clubs but you have the rest.

Back up to trick two. Say you lead a club to an honor and East DUCKS. You no longer can set up the club suit. East wins the second club and returns a heart. When the clubs fail to break you only have eight tricks.

If dummy has KQJxxx or AQJxxx facing xx in your hand and there is one side entry to dummy, make the same ducking play if you need FOUR tricks from the suit.

# CHAPTER 15

# ELIMINATION PLAYS, THROW-IN PLAYS, END PLAYS

A whole new vista of possibilities is open to you when you can draw trumps and still leave at least one trump in each hand. Side suits can be eliminated and opponents can be thrown in and forced to lead a particular suit or give you a ruff and a sluff.

364. When you have trump length in both hands and no long suit to establish for discards, there is a strong chance that you can execute some sort of end play. The simplest case is where there are losers in only one suit. No matter how weak the suit, STRIP THE HAND before you attack this suit. In the following example, the "only loser" suit is relatively strong.

> **North** (dummy)
> ♠ K3
> ♥ AQJ6
> ♦ 5432
> ♣ KQ10
>
> **South** (you)
> ♠ A5
> ♥ K10987
> ♦ AQ10
> ♣ A32

You arrive at a contract of six hearts and West leads the ♠Q. You have losers in only one suit, diamonds. Draw trumps, strip the black suits and lead a diamond to the ten. West will be endplayed upon winning the trick.

365. Do not make the fatal error of thinking that the only suit in which you have losers is so weak that it won't matter whether or not you strip the hand.

> **North** (dummy)
> 543
>
> **West**                                  **East**
> K9876                                QJ
>                 **South** (you)
>                 A102

Assume this is your only loser suit. If you strip the hand and play the ace and the deuce, either East wins and gives you a ruff and a sluff or West rises with the king, setting up your ten. Now consider this rather pathetic looking "only loser suit".

366.

| North (dummy) | |
|---|---|
| 543 | |

| West | East |
|---|---|
| A10987 | KQ |

South (you)
J62

The hand has been stripped. You have a trump on each side and this is the only suit in which you have losers. When you lead low from dummy, East-West cannot untangle themselves. The suit is blocked. After East wins two tricks, he must concede a ruff and a sluff.

367. Defenders who do not count are apt to make critical errors when a hand is stripped. You must give them every chance to shine.

North (dummy)
543

| West | East |
|---|---|
| Q7 | AK108 |

South (you)
J962

Assume the hand is stripped and you lead low from dummy. In order to take three tricks, East must play low. If East wins the trick, the suit is blocked and three defensive winners become two defensive winners.

368. After a hand has been stripped and you remain with one suit that may have as many as two or three losers (usually headed by the king or the ace-queen), try to duck the first loser into the hand that cannot safely return the suit.

North (dummy)
♠ 5432
♥ A6
♦ KJ984
♣ AQ

| West | East |
|---|---|
| ♠ K9 | ♠ J1076 |
| ♥ QJ104 | ♥ 9873 |
| ♦ 32 | ♦ 5 |
| ♣ J9876 | ♣ 10432 |

South (you)
♠ AQ8
♥ K52
♦ AQ1076
♣ K5

You arrive at the wonderful contract of six diamonds (your good bidding) and West leads the ♥Q. Your only losers are in spades so strip the hand before you lead a spade from dummy.

If East plays low, insert the eight endplaying West. If East plays the ten or the jack, win the ACE and return to dummy to lead a second spade to the queen. If West has the doubleton king, you still make the hand. West will have to give you a ruff and a sluff.

369. When you have losers in two suits, both equally divided between your hand and dummy, use the WEAKER as the throw-in suit to force a lead in the stronger.

North (dummy)
♠ A2
♥ AJ10
♦ KQ876
♣ KJ4

South (you)
♠ 87
♥ K54
♦ AJ1032
♣ AQ8

You contract is six diamonds and the lead is the ♠Q. You have losers in two suits, spades and hearts. Both are equally divided between the two hands. Spades are weaker so use that as your throw-in suit. Win the opening lead, draw trumps, strip the clubs and exit a spade. Whoever wins must lead a heart or concede a ruff and sluff.

370. If you have losers in two suits, one of which is equally divided and the other not, use the equally divided suit as your throw-in suit.

North (dummy)
♠ KQ76
♥ Q105
♦ K1032
♣ A4

South (you)
♠ AJ1098
♥ AK3
♦ A94
♣ 93

Your contract is six spades and the lead is the ♣Q. As you don't have time set up a diamond for a club discard, use the club loser to force a diamond play. Win the ♣A, draw trumps, strip the hearts and exit with a club. Whoever wins will either have to lead a diamond or concede a ruff and a sluff. If a diamond is led, play for split honors.

371. After a hand has been stripped and an opponent gives you a ruff and a sluff (instead of leading the "key suit"), DISCARD from the SHORT side of the key suit and ruff on the other side.

In the previous example, had the opponents played a third round of clubs, discard a diamond from your hand and ruff in dummy.

372. If you have two suits with losers including the trump suit, you may be able to use the trump suit as your throw-in suit.

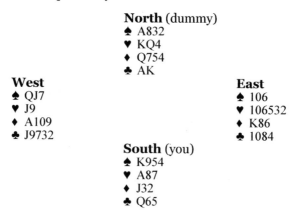

**North** (dummy)
♠ A832
♥ KQ4
♦ Q754
♣ AK

**West**
♠ QJ7
♥ J9
♦ A109
♣ J9732

**East**
♠ 106
♥ 106532
♦ K86
♣ 1084

**South** (you)
♠ K954
♥ A87
♦ J32
♣ Q65

Your contract is game in spades and West leads the ♣3. You have a spade loser as well as three possible diamond losers. If either opponent leads a

diamond you only have two diamond losers. Why not force them to lead a diamond?

Cash the ♠AK leaving the high trump at large and begin the stripping process. Cash a second club, return to your hand via a heart, cash the ♣Q discarding a diamond and continue with hearts. If the player with the high trump has not ruffed one of your winners, exit with a trump and force either a diamond return or a ruff and a sluff.

373. When stripping two suits with a high trump at large, STRIP THE SHORTER SUIT FIRST. In the previous example, clubs before hearts. If both suits have equal length, you may have to guess which suit to strip first. The object is to avoid a premature ruff followed by a safe exit.

374. If you don't have an equally divided suit with which to throw the opponents in, perhaps you can create one!

**North** (dummy)
♠ J3
♥ KJ1087
♦ KQ4
♣ J65

**South** (you)
♠ A75
♥ AQ95
♦ A3
♣ Q832

After you open one notrump and partner transfers, you wind up in four hearts with a low spade lead.

You have one spade loser and three possible club losers. Win the ♠A, draw trumps and discard a SPADE on the third diamond. Spades are now evenly divided between your hand and dummy. Exit a spade and force a club play.

375. The more balanced both hands are, the more endplays you can look forward to.

**North** (dummy)
♠ AJ76
♥ A32
♦ K104
♣ Q43

**West**
♠ 32
♥ KQ105
♦ Q876
♣ K92

**East**
♠ Q85
♥ 984
♦ 932
♣ A1087

**South** (you)
♠ K1094
♥ J76
♦ AJ5
♣ J65

You wind up in two spades and West leads the ♥K. Your hand and dummy have the identical distribution. Let the endplays begin!

Duck the opening lead. West is endplayed. Any suit that West leads either gives you a trick or obviates a guess. Assume West shifts to a trump. Play three rounds of trumps, then ace and a small heart. West, on play, is endplayed again.

376. It may not always be possible to strip a side suit entirely from both your hand and dummy. A partial strip is better than no strip at all!

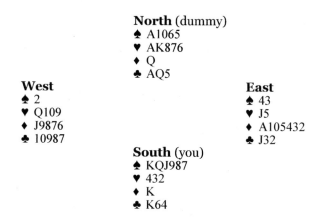

**North** (dummy)
♠ A1065
♥ AK876
♦ Q
♣ AQ5

**West**
♠ 2
♥ Q109
♦ J9876
♣ 10987

**East**
♠ 43
♥ J5
♦ A105432
♣ J32

**South** (you)
♠ KQJ987
♥ 432
♦ K
♣ K64

You arrive at a contract of six spades and West leads the ♣10. Draw trumps, strip the clubs, play two top hearts and exit a diamond. If the player with the ♦A has no more hearts, a ruff and a sluff will be coming your way. You will be able to discard your losing heart while ruffing in dummy.

377. Sometimes a hand can be stripped without drawing every opposing trump. If the player being thrown in does not have a safe trump exit, you will have pulled off a "partial" strip.

**North** (dummy)
♠ J98
♥ AJ108
♦ 1075
♣ KQ9

**West**
♠ 732
♥ 432
♦ J62
♣ 8765

**East**
♠ 54
♥ KQ7
♦ AK984
♣ 432

**South** (you)
♠ AKQ106
♥ 965
♦ Q3
♣ AJ10

You wind up in four spades after East deals and opens one diamond. West leads a low diamond and East continues with a second and third diamond which you ruff.

Chances are great that East has both heart honors. Draw TWO rounds of trumps, strip the clubs and lead a heart to the ten. Even though there is a trump outstanding, East does not have it. East is endplayed upon winning the trick. Contract made.

378. When you have two finesses to take, both known to be offside on the bidding, do not despair. If one of the two suits is equally divided, use that as your throw-in suit to avoid the finesse in the other suit.

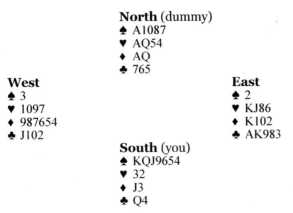

**North** (dummy)
- ♠ A1087
- ♥ AQ54
- ♦ AQ
- ♣ 765

**West**
- ♠ 3
- ♥ 1097
- ♦ 987654
- ♣ J102

**East**
- ♠ 2
- ♥ KJ86
- ♦ K102
- ♣ AK983

**South** (you)
- ♠ KQJ9654
- ♥ 32
- ♦ J3
- ♣ Q4

After East opens one club you wind up playing four spades. West leads the ♣J and the opponents play three rounds of clubs. With both red kings likely residing in the East hand, your best shot is a throw-in. Draw trump and

play the ace and queen of diamonds. East wins but any return gives you the balance.

379. Throwing an opponent in with a loser from one hand while discarding a loser from another is a "break even" play. However if the opponent that is thrown in must make a favorable return, you gain a trick.

**North** (dummy)
- ♠ 76
- ♥ KQ52
- ♦ AK4
- ♣ AQ32

**West**
- ♠ K542
- ♥ J1098
- ♦ 1092
- ♣ 74

**East**
- ♠ J1093
- ♥ 76
- ♦ 865
- ♣ J1098

**South** (you)
- ♠ AQ8
- ♥ A43
- ♦ QJ73
- ♣ K65

You wind up in 6NT and West leads the ♥J. You have eleven top tricks with high hopes for more if either the clubs or hearts break 3-3 or the spade finesse is on. Spades, your short suit, should be your LAST option. Win the heart in dummy, cash four diamonds, discarding a spade and test the clubs. When that suit does not break, test the hearts. No luck there either. However you have a cinch. Lead your losing heart and discard the eight of spades. West wins but must lead a spade into your AQ.

380. The concept of forcing a favorable return by leading a loser while discarding a loser is a common ploy at a suit contract as well. The idea is to strip a suit at the same time you are throwing one opponent on lead.

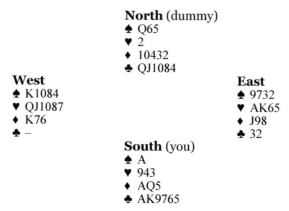

**North** (dummy)
♠ Q65
♥ 2
♦ 10432
♣ QJ1084

**West**
♠ K1084
♥ QJ1087
♦ K76
♣ —

**East**
♠ 9732
♥ AK65
♦ J98
♣ 32

**South** (you)
♠ A
♥ 943
♦ AQ5
♣ AK9765

After West shows the majors, you buy the hand for five clubs. West leads the ♥Q which is overtaken by the king and a spade is led to your ace. Your job is to avoid two diamond losers. Don't think finesse! Think, how can I avoid the finesse?

Ruff a heart, ruff a spade, ruff a heart (stripping that suit). Draw trump ending in dummy and lead the ♠Q, dummy's LAST spade. When East plays low, discard a diamond. West wins but must either lead a diamond into the AQ or give you a ruff and a sluff. Is your partner going to be impressed or what?

381. The true test of the recovering finesseaholic is if he can cast his eyes away from the finesse suit while asking, "Is there any way I can endplay somebody and avoid this finesse?"

**North** (dummy)
♠ AJ102
♥ 63
♦ K2
♣ AQJ104

**South** (you)
♠ KQ9876
♥ AJ
♦ A53
♣ 72

You arrive at six spades and West leads a heart to East's queen. The finessaholic wins, draws trump and takes the club finesse. It loses and East cashes the ♥K. The rehabilitated finessaholic draws trump, strips the diamonds and exits with a heart, the equally divided suit. If East wins the trick, no club finesse is needed. East is endplayed. If West takes the trick and leads a club, take the finesse. They do work every so often.

# CHAPTER 16

# COUNTING

The game begins and ends with counting. You must make a commitment to try to count each hand. Counting starts with the bidding. Whether you wind up as defender or declarer, it is important to make counting inferences from what the opponents bid and from what they DO NOT bid.

382. The more bids the opponents make, the easier it is to count the hand. With a little bit of luck you will know each player's distribution once the dummy comes down.

**North** (dummy)
- ♠ Q765
- ♥ 8765
- ♦ K5
- ♣ Q93

**South** (you)
- ♠ 832
- ♥ A
- ♦ A73
- ♣ AKJ1042

| West | North | East | South |
|------|-------|------|-------|
| 1♠ | Pass | 1NT | 2♣ |
| 2♥ | 3♣ | 3♦ | 5♣ |
| Pass | | | |

Opening lead: ♥K

West must have five spades missing the ace or king. With six spades, the suit would have been rebid and a high spade would have been led. Hearts must be 5-3. If East has four hearts, he would have supported. Diamonds? East must have six, perhaps seven. Therefore West is either 5-5-2-1 or 5-5-1-2. Are you too exhausted to play the hand? Draw two rounds of clubs, ruff a diamond, return to your hand by ruffing a heart, draw the last trump if necessary, and duck a spade to East's lone honor. Later, lead a spade to the queen.

383. Sometimes the count in one suit leads to an exact count in all four suits!

**North** (dummy)
♠ K543
♥ KQ93
♦ 5432
♣ 4

**South** (you)
♠ AJ7
♥ 102
♦ 87
♣ AK9532

| West | North | East | South |
|------|-------|------|-------|
| 1♦ | Pass | 2♦ | 3♣ |
| Pass | Pass | Pass | |

Opening lead: ♦K

Once you see six diamonds between your hand and dummy, you have a complete count on both hands! East would not raise a minor suit without at least four card support, so West must have three diamonds. If West has three diamonds, he should be 4-4 in the majors with a doubleton club. This might help you in the play to say the least!

384. Knowing the count of one suit can help with the count of another. Assume LHO opens one club and RHO responds one spade. If RHO turns up with four spades, it is safe to infer that he cannot have four hearts. With four hearts and four spades, the normal response is one heart.

385. It is usually not necessary to count both hands. Once a player either turns up with a long suit or has shown a long suit in the bidding, work with that hand. It makes life easier.

386. Watch the opponents' signals. In cases of ambiguity, a trusty high-low or low-high may clarify the position.

**North** (dummy)
♠ Q4
♥ AJ87
♦ AJ93
♣ J108

**South** (you)
♠ 6
♥ KQ1094
♦ K742
♣ AKQ

| South | West | North | East |
|-------|------|-------|------|
| 1♥    | 4♠   | 5♥    | Pass |
| Pass  | Pass |       |      |

Opening lead: ♠ K

West continues with the ♠A, East playing low-high. East's play indicates three spades, giving West seven. Ruff the second spade, draw trump and test the clubs. West turns up with a singleton trump and a singleton club.

The count is clear. West has started with a 7-1-4-1 pattern. Cash the ♦K and lead a low diamond to the nine.

387. Side suits that are missing a queen which can be finessed in either direction lend themselves to counting. Delay these finesses as long as possible in order to get either a complete or a partial count.

388. In general, if you have a two-way finesse for a jack or a queen, play the hand that is likely to have the greater length in the suit for the missing honor. With no information, finesse through the player you dislike the most. It's so much more fun when it works.

389. If the bidding marks an opponent with a particular honor but his partner has the greater length, make an exception and play the shorter hand for the missing honor.

390. When either opponent shows out of a suit, you have a complete count on that suit. Make a mental note of "showouts".

391. A good exercise in learning to count to 13 is to rattle off three small numbers to yourself such as two, three, two. Then ask yourself what number is missing to get the total to 13. This is exactly what you do when you count a hand. You may discover that one opponent has two cards in one suit, three in another and two in the third suit. Using higher mathematics you can deduce that the missing suit is six cards long.

392. It also helps if you can get a friend to call off three numbers to see if you can come up with that all important fourth number. Do not try this in public.

393. Defenders frequently give count signals in suits you initiate. Why not eavesdrop?

**North** (dummy)
Q1082

**West**
J765

**East**
94

**South** (you)
AK3

Say you need four tricks in this suit. Begin by leading the KING. Each defender may think his partner has the ace and give a count signal. In the diagram position, if each defender starts a high-low to show an even number of cards (or a low-high playing upside down count), you can cash the ace and lead low to the ten.

The key is NOT to let them see the ace on the first round of the suit. They are more apt to give an "honest count" when they each think their partner has the ace.

394. The size of the card led, particularly when an opponent leads his partner's suit, is revealing.

**North** (dummy)
♠A105

**West**
2

**East**

**South** (you)
♠K87

East opens one spade and West leads the 2♠. If E-W are playing 5 card majors, the lead must be a singleton.

If the suit in question is a minor, the more likely possibility is that East has four cards, West three, or vice versa.

395. When third hand bids a suit and does NOT overtake his partner's honor card lead, the inference is that third hand can not afford to overtake. This, in turn, makes it easier to count the suit.

**North** (dummy)
765

**West**
J

**East**
9

**South** (you)
♠A72

East opens one spade and West leads the jack and East plays the nine. The inference is that East does not have KQ109x(x) or else East would have overtaken. Play West for J10 doubleton.

396. Assuming fourth best leads, the lead of a low spot card followed by a lower spot card shows either a doubleton or a five card suit. Use the bidding and third hand play to guide you. If you can't tell the difference between a doubleton lead and a lead from a five card suit, there is always Bingo.

397. When the opponents lead third and fifth best, the lead of the lowest missing card indicates an odd number; three or five. The lead of a higher spot card followed by a lower spot card indicates an even number; usually two or four.

398. If the opening lead does not give you an exact count in a suit, third hand's second play of the suit usually will.

**North** (dummy)
976

**West**
2

**East**
(a) QJ4
(b) QJ43

**South** (you)
A85

The opponents, playing fourth best leads, lead the deuce. East plays the jack and you decide to duck. If East returns the queen (a), play East for three cards in the suit. If East returns the three (b), play East for four cards.

399. Sometimes the opening leader's second play in a suit will clarify the count.

**North** (dummy)
Q4

**West**
6

**East**

**South** (you)
103

East has preempted and West leads the six. The six could be top of a doubleton or low from three. Watch West's SECOND card. If it is lower assume a doubleton; if higher assume three.

400. Counting can even help you locate tens and jacks!

**North** (dummy)
KQ10x

**West**

**East**

**South** (you)
Axx

With no information, play king, ace, queen. However, if you can delay the play of this suit, you might get a count. For example, if you "knew" that West started with four cards in the suit, play king, ace and low to the ten. Besides, when you lead low to the king, the opponents might help you out by giving each other a count signal.

401. You can pull off some impressive finesses when you have the "count".

North (dummy)
KQ92

West
10876

East
J5

South (you)
A43

Assume you have delayed playing this suit until the bitter end. The count tells you that West started with four cards and East a doubleton. Play the king and back to the ace. If East plays either the ten or the jack, finesse the nine.

402. Sometimes you may attack a suit early and then delay later plays in the suit until you can get a count.

North (dummy)
KJ9x

West
(a) xxx
(b)10xxx

East
(a) Q10x
(b) Qx

South (you)
Axx

You begin by leading low to the jack and queen. If you can possibly delay a later play in the suit, you may discover that the suit was originally divided 3-3 (a). Alternatively, you may discover that "b" is the actual situation. Once you have the count, your follow up plays are a piece of cake.

403. Counting, plus keeping track of the spot cards, can pay big dividends.

North (dummy)
Q2

West
J8

East
K7543

South (you)
A1096

East opens the bidding in this suit and West leads the jack. You cover, East plays the king and you win. Later, West gets in and leads the eight to your ten. Finally, East gets in and leads a third round of the suit. At this point you have the 96 and East the 754. It is clear to play the six but just try to get

a non-counter or a non-lead watcher to play the six in this situation. Don't hold your breath.

404. Even the simplest of suit combinations can be affected by the count.

**North** (dummy)
- ♠ AQ4
- ♥ 108764
- ♦ AK
- ♣ 1043

**South** (you)
- ♠ KJ3
- ♥ AKQJ9
- ♦ 75
- ♣ A52

After East opens three diamonds, you become declarer at six hearts. West leads the nine of diamonds. What do you know? You know you have two club losers! You also know from both the bidding and the lead that diamonds are 7-2. You also know that when one hand is marked with a long suit, that is the hand to count.

You also know (or will know after you read the chapter on end plays) that when you have losers in only one suit you should strip the hand before you play that suit.

Draw trump and run the spades. East follows to two rounds of trump and two rounds of spades. Ergo, East started with two clubs. If those two clubs are the QJ, KJ or KQ, East can be endplayed by playing the ace and a club.

Had the count shown East with a singleton club, lead a LOW club instead of the ace. If East's lone club is an honor, whoever wins the club exit is endplayed.

# CHAPTER 17

# THE TRUMP SUIT

When playing a hand in a suit contract, there are any number of wondrous ways to squeeze out extra tricks. If you treat your trump suit with proper respect, you will be paid back a hundredfold.

## THE 4-4 TRUMP FIT

405. If both you and dummy have a singleton and neither you nor dummy has a powerful side suit, consider a crossruff.

**North** (dummy)
♠ AQ5
♥ 3
♦ AJ853
♣ KQ107

**South** (you)
♠ KJ7
♥ A8752
♦ 9
♣ AJ98

Your contract is six clubs and West leads the ♥K. You have two red aces and you can ruff four red cards in each hand for a grand total of 10 tricks. Therefore you need TWO spade tricks, not three. Play two rounds of spades and begin your crossruff.

In a contract of seven clubs cash THREE (or try to cash three) spades before crossruffing.

406. Before crossruffing, count the number of trump tricks you think you can score. This count tells you how many side suit winners you need.

407. Side suit winners are generally taken BEFORE crossruffing. They have the nasty habit of getting lost if you don't cash them early. Remember, opponents may be making discards while you are merrily crossruffing.

408. If you can take the same number of tricks at notrump as you can at your suit contract, convert to notrump at once. Do not fall into the trap of trumping a loser that can be discarded later.

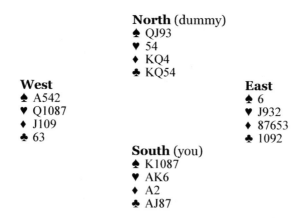

**North** (dummy)
- ♠ QJ93
- ♥ 54
- ♦ KQ4
- ♣ KQ54

**West**
- ♠ A542
- ♥ Q1087
- ♦ J109
- ♣ 63

**East**
- ♠ 6
- ♥ J932
- ♦ 87653
- ♣ 1092

**South** (you)
- ♠ K1087
- ♥ AK6
- ♦ A2
- ♣ AJ87

You arrive at six spades and West leads the ♦J. You have twelve notrump tricks. If you make the mistake of ruffing a heart in dummy (it can be discarded later on a diamond), down you go. West wins the THIRD round of spades and forces you to use your last trump by playing a fourth heart. West's fourth trump becomes the setting trick. Shame.

409. When trump divide 4-1 and you must take a ruff in one hand or the other, take the ruff in the hand that cannot be overruffed.

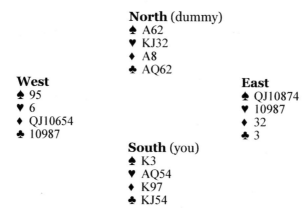

**North** (dummy)
- ♠ A62
- ♥ KJ32
- ♦ A8
- ♣ AQ62

**West**
- ♠ 95
- ♥ 6
- ♦ QJ10654
- ♣ 10987

**East**
- ♠ QJ10874
- ♥ 10987
- ♦ 32
- ♣ 3

**South** (you)
- ♠ K3
- ♥ AQ54
- ♦ K97
- ♣ KJ54

You wind up in seven hearts and West leads the ♦Q. You have twelve top tricks and if trump divide 3-2, you can ruff a diamond in dummy or a spade in your hand for your thirteenth trick. However you must cater to a possible 4-1 trump division. The key to drawing trump when there is a side suit that offers communication (clubs) is to begin by playing two rounds LEAVING A HIGH AND A LOW TRUMP in each hand.

When East turns up with heart length, ruff a spade in your hand, the suit East cannot overtrump. In contract of seven clubs, play the ♣AK. When West turns up with four clubs, play to ruff a diamond in dummy—the suit that West cannot overtrump.

410. When one hand has strong trump, the other weak, and both hands have shortness, ruff in the hand with the weaker trump holding. Conserve the stronger trump to draw their trump.

**North** (dummy)
♠ J654
♥ J952
♦ 54
♣ AK3

**South** (you)
♠ AKQ2
♥ 8763
♦ AK3
♣ 54

Four spades is the bid and the opponents begin by cashing three hearts and shifting to a club. As there is no problem if trump are 3-2, begin by cashing two rounds. This hand is different from the last, however. Here you do not have a side suit that has communications to both hands.

In order to allow for a possible 4-1 trump division, play the ace and the jack of spades. When the dreaded split occurs, ruff a diamond in dummy and return to your hand with dummy's last trump to draw trump. Had you started drawing trump by playing the AK (leaving a high and a low trump in each hand), you would not be able to draw trump after ruffing a diamond. The trump suit is blocked.

411. The weaker the side suit that you are establishing, the less likely you are to draw trump originally. The general rule is: side suit first, trumps later.

412. When each hand has a long side suit, it's usually right to set up the hand with the longer side suit.

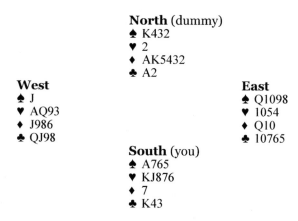

**North** (dummy)
- ♠ K432
- ♥ 2
- ♦ AK5432
- ♣ A2

**West**
- ♠ J
- ♥ AQ93
- ♦ J986
- ♣ QJ98

**East**
- ♠ Q1098
- ♥ 1054
- ♦ Q10
- ♣ 10765

**South** (you)
- ♠ A765
- ♥ KJ876
- ♦ 7
- ♣ K43

You arrive at four spades and West leads the ♣Q. Establish diamonds, not hearts. Win the opening lead in your hand (conserving dummy entries) and play the ♦A and ruff a diamond. Continue by cashing the ♠AK. Even if spades are 4-1, you are O.K. Ruff another diamond, cross to a club and play high diamonds. The most you can lose is two spades and one heart.

413. If a contract is so good that it can stand a 4-1 trump division, play for a 4-1 split. If a contract is so fragile that it cannot withstand a 4-1 trump break, play for a 3-2 division.

414. When playing a DOUBLED contract holding a plethora of outside aces and kings, count on this: TRUMPS ARE NOT BREAKING 3-2. If you are LUCKY, they will be divided "only" 4-1. (End of discussion of 4-4 trump fits).

415. In order to retain control of the trump suit, do not allow an opponent to wind up with more trump than you. It is decidedly unhealthy.

416. By voiding a side suit in BOTH your hand and dummy, you make it impossible for the opponents to lead that suit without giving you a ruff and a sluff. In addition, the opponents cannot force you to trump in the long hand by leading the voided suit. You can always take the ruff in the short hand. The idea of voiding a side suit in both hands is one of the guiding principles of trump control.

417. No law says that when the opponents lead a suit in which you have a loser, and dummy is void in that suit that you have to ruff in dummy.

1) You may need dummy's trump as a way to get back to your hand.

**North** (dummy)
♠ 8
♥ A765
♦ AKQ432
♣ Q5

**South** (you)
♠ AKQJ102
♥ 43
♦ 65
♣ 876

You wind up in four spades after West has overcalled two clubs. West leads the ♣AKJ, East playing high-low. Although it may be tempting to ruff in dummy, don't! If East overtrumps and returns a heart, how will you get off dummy to draw trump? (Something to think about BEFORE you play) If you discard a low diamond or a low heart from dummy on the third club, the rest of the tricks are yours.

418. (2) When there is a danger that the dummy will be overruffed and a loser can be discarded instead of ruffing, discard the loser.

**North** (dummy)
♠ 8765
♥ A32
♦ Q3
♣ K876

**South** (you)
♠ AKQ104
♥ K65
♦ 987
♣ A3

Again you are playing four spades. This time West has overcalled two diamonds. West leads the ♦AKJ, East playing high-low. Rather than ruff the third diamond and risk an overruff, discard a heart. After trumps have been removed, you can ruff a heart. Play the same if dummy has ♥AJx.

419. (3) If ruffing will remove a vital dummy entry prematurely, decline the ruff.

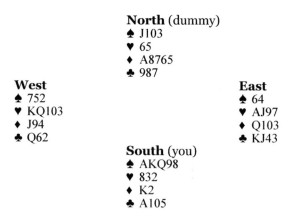

**North** (dummy)
- ♠ J103
- ♥ 65
- ♦ A8765
- ♣ 987

**West**
- ♠ 752
- ♥ KQ103
- ♦ J94
- ♣ Q62

**East**
- ♠ 64
- ♥ AJ97
- ♦ Q103
- ♣ KJ43

**South** (you)
- ♠ AKQ98
- ♥ 832
- ♦ K2
- ♣ A105

Once again you are in four spades (how did you get so high?) and the opponents lead three rounds of hearts. If you ruff, you are doomed to lose two more club tricks.

Dummy's third trump is needed as a LATER entry to the diamonds. Discard a club on the third heart and hope diamonds divide 3-3. Win the club return, establish the diamonds with one ruff and draw three rounds of trump ENDING in dummy. Discard the losing clubs on the established diamonds.

420. It is useless to establish a side suit in either hand if you don't have an entry to use the suit. If the only entries are in the trump suit, DON'T DRAW TRUMP until the side suit has been established.

**North** (dummy)
- ♠ J10
- ♥ QJ98
- ♦ K54
- ♣ A105

**South** (you)
- ♠ Q987
- ♥ AK107
- ♦ 76
- ♣ 986

You arrive at three hearts (everybody else is in two hearts), and the lead is the ♦Q. After you ruff the third diamond, establish spades. Your plan is to discard both of dummy's clubs on the two established spades. With careful play you will lose two spades and two diamonds. It is a major blunder to draw trump first. How will you get back to the spades?

421. When you wind up in a four level contract missing the AK of trump (with a 10 card fit) plus two quick side suit losers, call in the magicians.

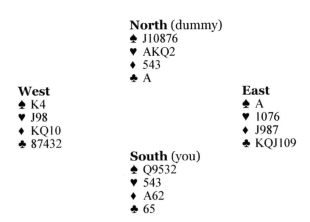

**North** (dummy)
- ♠ J10876
- ♥ AKQ2
- ♦ 543
- ♣ A

**West**
- ♠ K4
- ♥ J98
- ♦ KQ10
- ♣ 87432

**East**
- ♠ A
- ♥ 1076
- ♦ J987
- ♣ KQJ109

**South** (you)
- ♠ Q9532
- ♥ 543
- ♦ A62
- ♣ 65

After East opens one club, you wind up in four spades. West leads the ♦K and you are in serious trouble. What, you think you have to lose four tricks? No way, Jose. Win the ace of diamonds and play four rounds of hearts discarding a diamond. East dare not ruff the fourth heart, so West ruffs. Once West ruffs, the top trumps collide. You lose two trump tricks but only one diamond. What if hearts are not 3-3? Have you never gone set before?

## MANAGING A POSSIBLE FOURTH ROUND SIDE SUIT LOSER

422. Trump suit finesses for a queen that may preclude ruffing a possible fourth round loser in dummy are normally shunned.

**North** (dummy)
- ♠ 432
- ♥ 865
- ♦ AK32
- ♣ AK5

**West**
- ♠ Q109
- ♥ 93
- ♦ QJ109
- ♣ Q1043

**East**
- ♠ 87
- ♥ J1074
- ♦ 874
- ♣ J972

**South** (you)
- ♠ AKJ65
- ♥ AKQ2
- ♦ 65
- ♣ 86

You are declarer in six spades and West leads the ♦Q. You have two concerns: the trump suit and the FOURTH heart. If you play for a 3-2 trump split (68%), you are home free. Win the opening lead and cash the ♠AK leaving the queen at large. Now attack hearts. Cash the AKQ. If the ♠Q trumps one of your heart winners, no big deal. You can still ruff your ♥2 with dummy's mighty ♠4.

When the smoke clears, you have lost one trick. If you take the trump finesse and it loses, you may not be able to ruff your fourth heart safely. The player with the doubleton heart may have three spades.

423. With a trump suit of xxxxx(x) facing Axx plus a fourth round loser that must be trumped in dummy, duck a trump, play the ace and then ruff the loser.

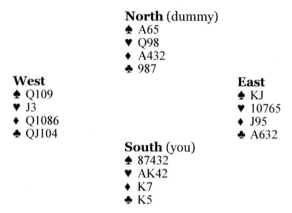

**North** (dummy)
- ♠ A65
- ♥ Q98
- ♦ A432
- ♣ 987

**West**
- ♠ Q109
- ♥ J3
- ♦ Q1086
- ♣ QJ104

**East**
- ♠ KJ
- ♥ 10765
- ♦ J95
- ♣ A632

**South** (you)
- ♠ 87432
- ♥ AK42
- ♦ K7
- ♣ K5

The contract is four spades and West leads the ♣Q to East's ace. East returns a club. With two certain trump losers, you must make provision for that fourth heart. Duck a trump, ruff the club return and play the ♠A leaving the master trump at large. Now go about your business of trumping the fourth heart in dummy.

424. When you have a third and a possible fourth round loser in a side suit (Axx facing Kxxx or AKxx facing xxx) and there is a HIGH trump in dummy which you can afford to use as a ruffer, play the AK and concede a trick in the side suit EARLY. If the side suit does not break 3-3, trump the fourth card with dummy's high trump.

**North** (dummy)
- ♠ A32
- ♥ K32
- ♦ 987
- ♣ A432

**South** (you)
- ♠ KQJ104
- ♥ A765
- ♦ 54
- ♣ K7

You wind up in four spades. The opponents begin with three rounds of diamonds, you ruffing the third. Your major concern must be your FOURTH heart as one heart must be lost in any event.

Fortunately you have a high trump in dummy. Play two top hearts and concede a heart. If the fourth heart is not high, trump it with the ♠A.

425. When your side suit has a third and possible fourth round loser and you are cursed with only low trump in the dummy, a different technique must be used. DUCK the FIRST ROUND of the side suit, draw TWO rounds of trump and then try to trump your fourth round loser in dummy.

**North** (dummy)
♠ 532
♥ 432
♦ 987
♣ A432

**South** (you)
♠ AKQJ10
♥ AK65
♦ 54
♣ K7

The contract is four spades and the opponents begin by playing three rounds of diamonds.

The problem is your *&%$# fourth heart. This time you are stuck with only LOW trumps in dummy. DUCK a heart, win any return and play the ♠AK, leaving a LOW trump at large, and cash the ♥AK. If hearts divide 3-3, draw the remaining trump and claim. If hearts are 4-2, hope (pray) that the player with the odd trump also has four hearts. If so, you can ruff your heart in dummy.

If the player with the two hearts has the odd trump, tomorrow is another day.

426. If you suspect there may be a foul division in a side suit, the safest way to cash winners in that suit is to lead TOWARD those winners. Do not lead the winners outright. It is somewhat akin to leading a lamb to slaughter.

**North** (dummy)
76

**West**
Q10854

**East**
J

**South** (you)
AK932

This is a side suit in a trump contract and you wish to ruff several of your losers in dummy. The bad news is that West has bid the suit and East has a likely singleton. Cash the ace, enter dummy in another suit and lead toward the king. If East ruffs, he ruffs air (a loser). If East doesn't ruff, you score your king. If you have reason to believe that East is VOID, lead twice from dummy toward your AK.

427. In order to keep control of both your trump suit and your long suit, conceding a potential trump loser early (while keeping a trump in the dummy) may be the answer.

**North** (dummy)
♠ K43
♥ —
♦ AKQJ98
♣ A765

**South** (you)
♠ AJ1098
♥ 98543
♦ 102
♣ 9

You arrive at a contract of six spades and West leads a high heart, ruffed in dummy. You have reached a common position: possible trump loser, running side suit, beaucoup losers in dummy's short suit. The answer is to take an EARLY trump finesse. Even if the finesse loses, you have a trump in dummy to protect yourself against a heart return.

At trick two, lead a LOW spade to the jack. If the jack holds, return to the ♠K, cash the ♣A and ruff a club; draw the last trump and score up an overtrick. If the finesse loses, regardless of the return, you have the rest. If trumps are 4-1 and the ♠J wins, you are in big trouble. In that case, inform your partner he should have insisted on diamonds as the trump suit. If your spades were AQ109x instead of AJ109x, lead a low spade to the ten at trick two. This locks up your contract if either defender has four spades to the jack.

428. Another guiding principle to avoid a long hand force: when both you and dummy are void in the same suit and a trump trick must be lost, try to concede your trump loser while at least one trump REMAINS in dummy.

**North** (dummy)
- ♠ 932
- ♥ 543
- ♦ 876
- ♣ 9876

**West**
- ♠ K874
- ♥ KQ102
- ♦ 932
- ♣ J2

**East**
- ♠ 5
- ♥ AJ98
- ♦ J1054
- ♣ 10543

**South** (you)
- ♠ AQJ106
- ♥ 76
- ♦ AKQ
- ♣ AKQ

Can you handle one more four spade contract? Look at that beautiful dummy! The opponents begin with three rounds of hearts reducing you to four trump. Rather than subject yourself to another possible heart force, exit with the ♠Q. If that holds, play the ♠J. West can win the king either time but cannot force you with a heart as long as one trump remains in dummy. (If West ducks twice, play the ♠A and run your minor suit winners). If you carelessly play the ace and queen of spades at tricks four and five, West ducks, wins the third spade and punches you with a fourth heart. Curtains.

429. In order to avoid a long hand force it may be necessary to discard a seemingly worthless card from dummy before either drawing trump or establishing side suit winners. (The "double void" principle).

**North** (dummy)
- ♠ 932
- ♥ 72
- ♦ 8765
- ♣ AQJ5

**West**
- ♠ K876
- ♥ J98
- ♦ AKQ10
- ♣ 92

**East**
- ♠ 5
- ♥ 106543
- ♦ J98
- ♣ 1073

**South** (you)
- ♠ AQJ104
- ♥ AKQ
- ♦ 42
- ♣ K84

West opens one diamond and you forge on to four spades. West leads three rounds of diamonds reducing you to the same trump length as West (although you don't know that). It may seem right to draw trump, but it isn't! If you cross to a club and take a spade finesse, West wins and punches you with a fourth diamond. A big no-no has just taken place. West has more trump than you do.

In order to protect yourself from a second force in diamonds, play three rounds of hearts and discard dummy's last diamond. With both your hand and dummy void in diamonds, exit with the ♠Q. If West wins, he cannot force you in diamonds (dummy takes the force) and, if West ducks, continue with the ♠J. West has no defense.

## PLAYING THE DREADED 4-3 TRUMP FIT

Do not fear a 4-3 trump fit. They present interesting play problems. (Some experienced players are still afraid to play a 4-3 trump fit!) One of your main concerns is to keep control of the trump suit, particularly when one opponent has four trump. In the meantime the defense is doggedly trying to shorten your trump holding.

430. When playing a marginal 4-3 trump fit, it helps ENORMOUSLY to have the ace of trump in one of the two hands.

431. One technique to avoid a "long hand force" is to discard losers from your hand while patiently waiting for dummy to be void in the "force suit". Once the dummy is void, the long hand is "safe".

**North** (dummy)
♠ 543
♥ 765
♦ A843
♣ Q95

**South** (you)
♠ —
♥ AKQJ
♦ J752
♣ AKJ108

Faced with a spade lead against your four heart contract, you are presented with the classic problem of how to draw trump and enjoy your club suit. As trump figure to be 4-2, it is decidedly unhealthy to ruff in your hand. Discard three diamonds on the first three spade leads. If the opponents persist in spades, ruff in dummy, draw trump and get on to the next hand.

432. Kxx opposite Axxx is a touchy trump suit at best. After the long hand has been forced once, it becomes even touchier. Ducking a round of trump is the best way to begin to draw trump.

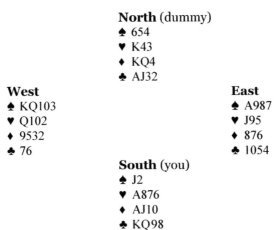

**North** (dummy)
♠ 654
♥ K43
♦ KQ4
♣ AJ32

**West**
♠ KQ103
♥ Q102
♦ 9532
♣ 76

**East**
♠ A987
♥ J95
♦ 876
♣ 1054

**South** (you)
♠ J2
♥ A876
♦ AJ10
♣ KQ98

Fearing notrump because of the spade weakness, you alight in four hearts. The opponents begin with three rounds of spades. As you have a certain trump loser, you must accept the force. You are now reduced to playing for a 3-3 trump division. Even so, you cannot play three rounds of hearts. Whoever wins will cash a spade. The only way out of this quagmire is to duck a heart. If the opponents persist with a fourth spade, ruff in either hand, draw trump and move once again to the next hand.

433. When your ONLY losers are in the trump suit and there is a danger of being shortened, ask yourself how many trump tricks you can afford to lose. If you can arrange to leave exactly that number of trump at large before playing your winners, that is the play.

**North** (dummy)
♠ 642
♥ 5432
♦ AQ4
♣ KJ9

**West**
♠ Q1098
♥ J1098
♦ 86
♣ 865

**East**
♠ J3
♥ A76
♦ 10972
♣ 10732

**South** (you)
♠ AK75
♥ KQ
♦ KJ53
♣ AQ4

After partner missorts his cards (is there no end to the mistakes he makes?), you become declarer in four spades and the opponents lead the ♥J to the ace and a heart is returned.

Your only losers are in the trump suit and you can afford to lose two trump tricks. In addition you do not want to shorten the long hand. Play the ♠AK leaving two trump at large and begin to play winners. You lose the expected two trump tricks.

434. When dealing with a solid side suit in dummy (the good news), but no outside dummy entry (the bad news), the idea is to draw ALL the trump before attacking the side suit. This may require ducking one round of trump in order to (1) retain control of the trump suit; (2) avoid a force; (3) both of the above.

**North** (dummy)
♠ 743
♥ 743
♦ AKQJ10
♣ 82

**West**
♠ 985
♥ 96
♦ 984
♣ KQ1075

**East**
♠ QJ10
♥ J1052
♦ 65
♣ AJ93

**South** (you)
♠ AK62
♥ AKQ8
♦ 732
♣ 64

You have arrived at four hearts. The opponents begin with two rounds of clubs and shift to a spade. In order to run the diamonds in peace, win the spade and duck a heart taking out insurance against a 4-2 break. The best the opponents can do is continue with a second spade. You win, draw trump and run the diamonds. Nothing to this game.

If you play the AKQ of hearts at tricks four, five and six, you are in big trouble. You can't afford to give up a heart so you must switch your attention to diamonds. East ruffs the third diamond and forces you to use your last trump with a third club. How does down two grab you in a cold contract? End of discussion of 4-3 fits.

435. There are times when you have to expose yourself to a ruff by attacking a side suit BEFORE drawing all the enemy trump. However you may be able to hedge a bit and draw SOME trump.

**North** (dummy)
♠ 763
♥ A42
♦ A543
♣ QJ10

**West**
♠ AKJ5
♥ 753
♦ 72
♣ A876

**East**
♠ Q10864
♥ 96
♦ 1086
♣ K95

**South** (you)
♠ 9
♥ KQJ108
♦ KQJ9
♣ 432

West opens one club and after some mild spade bidding by the opponents, you wind up in four hearts. West begins with two high spades forcing you to ruff.

The average player (your partner) draws trump, runs the diamonds and then tries to set up a tenth trick in clubs. No luck. After the opponents win the first club and play a third spade, your partner has just run out of trump! When your partner plays a second club, whoever wins cashes the setting trick in spades.

You, of course, draw TWO rounds of trumps before attacking clubs. The opponents win and play a spade reducing you to one trump in each hand, West also clutching a trump. When you play a second club, the opponents are helpless. You have retained control and you have the balance of the tricks.

436. When the dummy has a king in a suit in which you are void, you may not be too thrilled to be constantly attacked in this suit. The idea is to keep the hand that can lead through the king off play as long as possible.

**North** (dummy)
♠ AJ7
♥ K5432
♦ 32
♣ AJ10

**West**
♠ 862
♥ QJ109
♦ A965
♣ 93

**East**
♠ K953
♥ A876
♦ 4
♣ 7542

**South** (you)
♠ Q104
♥ —
♦ KQJ1087
♣ KQ86

Showing no respect for partner's opening one heart bid, West leads the ♥Q against your five diamond contract. You play low from dummy and ruff in your hand.

As you may have to drive out two cards, the ♦A and the ♠K, there is some danger of repeated heart forces (trumps may be 4-1). Take the spade finesse first. This finesse goes into the non-danger hand—East, the player who cannot conveniently attack hearts. If you play diamonds before spades, a second heart force reduces you to West's trump length. When East gets in with the ♠K, a third heart play destroys you.

437. When you are forced to trump in the short hand, be careful not to block the trump suit.

**North** (dummy)
♠ —
♥ AKQ43
♦ AQJ6
♣ AQJ6

**West**
♠ AKJ85
♥ J8
♦ 942
♣ K75

**East**
♠ Q109632
♥ 10752
♦ 1083
♣ —

**South** (you)
♠ 74
♥ 96
♦ K75
♣ 1098432

You are playing a contract of seven clubs and West leads a high spade. Ruff with an honor in dummy so that you can return to your hand with a diamond to run the ♣10 through West. If you ruff low, you will need TWO hand entries to take two club finesses. You only have one. Sorry about that.

438. Have you ever been in this predicament? You can't afford to lose any more tricks and there is a known finesseable trump honor to your right. But alas! no trump in dummy to take the finesse. Do not despair. A trump coup may be in your future. The two keys are: (1) reduce your trump length to that of your opponent; (2) wind up in the dummy at trick ELEVEN.

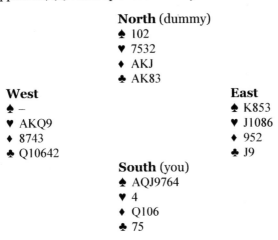

**North** (dummy)
♠ 102
♥ 7532
♦ AKJ
♣ AK83

**West**
♠ –
♥ AKQ9
♦ 8743
♣ Q10642

**East**
♠ K853
♥ J1086
♦ 952
♣ J9

**South** (you)
♠ AQJ9764
♥ 4
♦ Q106
♣ 75

You wind up in six spades after partner discovers your heart shortness. (Don't ask how; this is a book on play).

Ruff the second heart, cross to dummy with a diamond and run the ♠10. The good news is the finesse works. The bad news is that East remains with three spades and dummy only has one. The ♠K is not finesseable. You must go for a trump coup. Repeat the spade finesse, cross to dummy with a club and ruff another heart. You remain with three trump, East has two. Your work isn't over. Return to dummy with a club and ruff another heart, finally reducing yourself to the same length as East. Play two more rounds of diamonds ending in dummy at trick eleven. You must take the last two tricks with the ♠AQ.

Is your partner going to believe this? Are you? Is anybody?

439. Trump coups require foresight. You must anticipate possible bad breaks in the trump suit and begin the shortening process early...just in case.

**North** (dummy)
♠ 42
♥ A743
♦ AK92
♣ 1084

**West**
♠ 6
♥ KQJ92
♦ 65
♣ J6532

**East**
♠ J875
♥ 1086
♦ 8743
♣ 97

**South** (you)
♠ AKQ1093
♥ 5
♦ QJ10
♣ AKQ

The contract is seven spades and West leads the ♥K. Having been victimized by one too many 4-1 trump breaks, you ruff a heart at trick two just in case. When you continue with the ♠AK and West shows out, you have another chance to shine. As East needs at least three diamonds for your coup to succeed, lead the ♦Q to the king and ruff a second heart reducing to East's trump length. Cash the AK of clubs, the ♦J and overtake the ♦10. When East turns up with four diamonds, play dummy's high diamond, the nine, and discard your last club.

There you are again in dummy at trick eleven hovering over East's trump holding. Lead anything from dummy and take the last two tricks.

What if East had only three diamonds? You would still play your fourth diamond leaving East with no good answer. If East ruffs, overruff, draw the last trump and your third club is high. If East discards, discard your last club and wind up in dummy at trick eleven.

440. If you can't arrange to end up in dummy at the eleventh trick to execute a trump coup, having either opponent on lead at trick eleven will work just as well, thank you.

**North** (dummy)
♠ A875
♥ K876
♦ 643
♣ 63

**West**
♠ J1093
♥ J932
♦ 10875
♣ 2

**East**
♠ KQ62
♥ Q10
♦ J92
♣ J987

**South** (you)
♠ 4
♥ A54
♦ AKQ
♣ AKQ1054

West leads the ♠J against your neat contract of six clubs. Again, one of the things that can go wrong is if East has four clubs to the jack. (If West has Jxxx, there is not much you can do). Showing class, you ruff a spade at trick two and continue with two top trump. When West shows out on the second trump, you have your work cut out for you. Cash three diamonds and two hearts ending in dummy. So far so good. Next, ruff a spade reducing to the same trump length as East. The stage is set. Exit with a heart at trick ten giving the opponents the lead at trick eleven. You must take the last two tricks with the ♣Q10.

441. It is usually right to defer leading up to a KJ suit as long as possible in order to get more "honor" information. However when the "force is on" and you need a quick trick, you may have to lead the suit early.

**North** (dummy)
♠ KJ52
♥ A3
♦ 875
♣ K1094

**South** (you)
♠ 76
♥ KQJ105
♦ J10
♣ AQJ3

Your contract is four hearts. The opponents get off to the strong defense of three rounds of diamonds. (It appears that West started with KQxx and East Axxx). You ruff the diamond and take stock. You have nine winners in hearts and clubs and need a tenth in spades. If you draw trumps before attacking spades it may be too late. If hearts are 4-2, you won't have any trump left when you lead a spade. Not good.

Whoever has the ♠A will win the trick and cash a fourth diamond. You must lead a spade BEFORE you draw trump. If West plays low, which spade should you play? The right one of course.

442.  Each ruff in the short hand is worth one extra trick. Ruffing in the long hand is a horse of another color. In order to secure an extra trick by ruffing in the long hand you must ruff enough times so that the short hand becomes the long hand! If you are playing a 5-3 trump fit, you must ruff THREE times in the long hand leaving the dummy with one more trump than you. This is the principle behind the "dummy reversal".

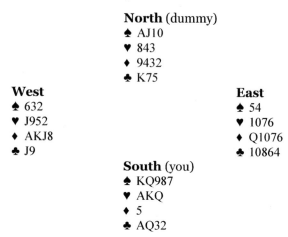

**North** (dummy)
- ♠ AJ10
- ♥ 843
- ♦ 9432
- ♣ K75

**West**
- ♠ 632
- ♥ J952
- ♦ AKJ8
- ♣ J9

**East**
- ♠ 54
- ♥ 1076
- ♦ Q1076
- ♣ 10864

**South** (you)
- ♠ KQ987
- ♥ AKQ
- ♦ 5
- ♣ AQ32

You arrive at the superior contract of six spades but now you have to play it. West begins by leading two top diamonds. Count tricks. You have five spades, three hearts and three clubs. In addition, you can make an extra trick if clubs break 3-3. Or you can draw two rounds of trump and then try to ruff your fourth club in dummy. This play requires that the hand with four clubs also has the long trump...against the odds. A better plan is to ruff THREE diamonds in your hand, giving you a total of SIX trump tricks to go along with three hearts and three clubs.

Cross to a club and ruff a diamond. Return to the ten of spades and ruff dummy's last diamond. Overtake your last trump and discard your losing club on partner's last trump. Your hand is high. Your dummy reversal needed a 3-2 trump division (68%).

443.  There are at least five ways to try to avoid an adverse ruff. You can (1) "fake" a trump finesse.

**North** (dummy)
K93

**West**          **East**
A5               64

**South** (you)
QJ10872

With the lead in your own hand and fearing the possibility of an adverse ruff, lead the jack of trump. If West ducks, there will be no adverse ruffing.

444.  You can (2) discard the suit that they can ruff before they regain the lead.

**North** (dummy)
♠ A74
♥ Q86
♦ 962
♣ A1062

**West**                              **East**
♠ QJ109853                           ♠ 2
♥ A                                  ♥ 742
♦ 5                                  ♦ 10743
♣ Q987                               ♣ KJ543

**South** (you)
♠ K6
♥ KJ10953
♦ AKQJ8
♣ —

After West opens four spades and you fight back with five hearts which partner cheerfully raises to six hearts. West leads the ♠Q. Be careful! Think first, play later.

The obvious danger is that East has a singleton spade and West the ace of hearts. In this, the ugliest of all scenarios, West wins the ♥A and gives East a spade ruff. You have an answer. Win the ace of spades and discard the king of spades on the ace of clubs. Now it is safe to draw trumps.

445.  You can (3) strip the hand before giving up the lead. The player who eventually gets a ruff may be endplayed.

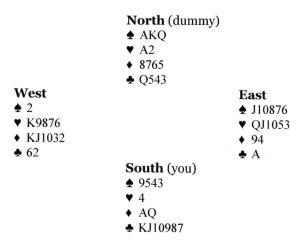

**North** (dummy)
♠ AKQ
♥ A2
♦ 8765
♣ Q543

**West**
♠ 2
♥ K9876
♦ KJ1032
♣ 62

**East**
♠ J10876
♥ QJ1053
♦ 94
♣ A

**South** (you)
♠ 9543
♥ 4
♦ AQ
♣ KJ10987

After partner opens a strong notrump and East shows a major two-suiter, you buy the hand for five clubs. West leads an ominous ♠2. Be careful! Think first, play later. The danger is that West will get a spade ruff and you may later lose a diamond. The solution is to strip the hearts before leading a trump. When East gets in with the ace of trumps, he does indeed give West a spade ruff. However West is endplayed. West must either lead a diamond into your AQ or concede a ruff and a sluff with an equally disastrous result.

446. You can (4) transfer the entry from the player who can give his partner a ruff to the one who can't.

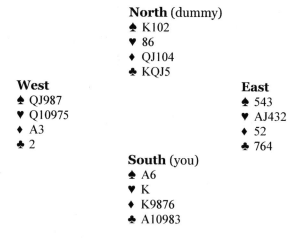

**North** (dummy)
♠ K102
♥ 86
♦ QJ104
♣ KQJ5

**West**
♠ QJ987
♥ Q10975
♦ A3
♣ 2

**East**
♠ 543
♥ AJ432
♦ 52
♣ 764

**South** (you)
♠ A6
♥ K
♦ K9876
♣ A10983

You open one diamond, West overcalls two diamonds to show the majors, partner cue bids two spades. East leaps to four hearts and you wind up in five diamonds. Once again an ominous ♣2 hits the table. What is likely to happen? If West has the ♦A and East the ♥A, West will win the trump ace, lead a heart to East's ace and get a club ruff.

What can you do to prevent this? You must make it impossible for West to put East in with the ♥A. How? Play three rounds of spades. If East cannot cover the ♠10, discard your heart. An "entry exchange". West wins but cannot get to East for the club ruff. Bravo, you have just executed a "scissors coup".

447. You can (5) give your opponent the impression that no ruff is pending by throwing away a winner while clutching a loser!

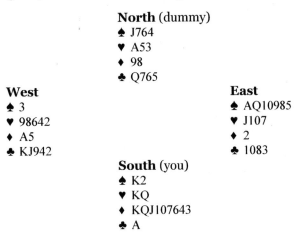

**North** (dummy)
♠ J764
♥ A53
♦ 98
♣ Q765

**West**
♠ 3
♥ 98642
♦ A5
♣ KJ942

**East**
♠ AQ10985
♥ J107
♦ 2
♣ 1083

**South** (you)
♠ K2
♥ KQ
♦ KQJ107643
♣ A

After East opens two spades (weak), you wind up playing five diamonds. West leads the ♠3, an obvious singleton. After East wins the ♠A, drop the king. Most Easts on this planet will think that West has led from the ♠32. Once East does not continue a spade, the contract cannot be defeated.

448. You can (6) ruff your own winner high before they ruff it low.

**North** (dummy)
- ♠ 653
- ♥ 93
- ♦ K4
- ♣ AJ6543

**West**
- ♠ 82
- ♥ 765
- ♦ J9876
- ♣ Q98

**East**
- ♠ AQ1097
- ♥ A42
- ♦ 1032
- ♣ K10

**South** (you)
- ♠ KJ4
- ♥ KQJ108
- ♦ AQ5
- ♣ 72

After East opens one spade you and your partner cleverly avoid the laydown 3NT to arrive at the reasonable four hearts. West leads a spade to the ace followed by a second spade to your jack. Can you see it coming? When you lead a trump, East will win the ace and give West a spade ruff. You still have a club loser so this line of play translates to down one.

What you must do is immediately play three rounds of diamonds discarding dummy's remaining spade. Now ruff your good ♠K with dummy's ♥9. So much for losing your ♠K. But what if dummy doesn't have the ♥9?

Would I do that to you while you are suffering through this chapter?

449. If an enemy crossruff is looming or if dummy has a long side suit with no outside entry, it is probably best to play the hand at notrump.

**North** (dummy)
- ♠ A4
- ♥ AQ7654
- ♦ 86
- ♣ 843

**South** (you)
- ♠ KQJ1076
- ♥ 32
- ♦ AJ
- ♣ AK9

After partner opens with a rather emaciated one heart, you end up in six spades. You get a temporary reprieve when West leads the ♣Q. As there is no point in trying to ruff a heart to set up the suit (no side entry), play as if the contract were 6NT. Win the opening lead, draw trumps, and duck a heart. Win any return and take the heart finesse. Play the same if dummy's hearts were AKxxxx.

450. Clever defenders are always on the prowl for extra trump tricks. One of their favorite techniques is the "uppercut". This is what you must be on the lookout to avoid.

**North** (dummy)
843

**West**
Q109

**East**
J2

**South** (you)
AK765

Assume spades are trump and both you and East are void in hearts. If West leads a heart and East "uppercuts" you with the jack, your one loser trump suit has suddenly become a two loser trump suit.

451. One defense to an "uppercut" is to refuse to overtrump, discarding a loser or a possible loser instead.

Dealer West
Both sides vul.

**North** (dummy)
♠ 765
♥ 1043
♦ K965
♣ KQJ

**West**
♠ 1094
♥ AKJ652
♦ 83
♣ 76

**East**
♠ K3
♥ Q9
♦ QJ102
♣ 109832

**South** (you)
♠ AQJ82
♥ 87
♦ A74
♣ A54

| West | North | East | South |
|------|-------|------|-------|
| 2♥* | Pass | 3♥** | 3♠ |
| Pass | 4♠ | Pass | Pass |

\* Weak
\*\* Preemptive

Opening lead: ♥K

West continues with the ace and a LOW heart (asking, begging East to uppercut). East obliges by ruffing with the trump king. If you overruff, you are doomed to lose a later trump trick as well as a diamond trick. Better to discard a diamond, a certain loser on the ♠K. If you do, you wind up making your contract losing two hearts and a spade.

452. If the opponents lead a suit in which you have the ace in dummy opposite a singleton in your hand, you are under no moral obligation to play the ace...particularly when there is a good chance it will be ruffed.

**North** (dummy)
♠ A876
♥ K32
♦ J1087
♣ 32

**South** (you)
♠ 3
♥ A84
♦ AKQ532
♣ A87

After you open one diamond and West overcalls four spades, you become declarer in a contract of five diamonds.

West leads the ♠K.

As there is an excellent chance that East is void in spades, play low from dummy at trick one. Later you can discard your losing heart on the ♠A. You wind up losing a spade and a club. If you play the ♠A at trick one and East ruffs, you wind up losing a heart, a club and the ruff.

453. When you are sure an opponent is going to ruff one of your winners and this winner cannot be ruffed on the next lead of the suit, conserve the winner for later.

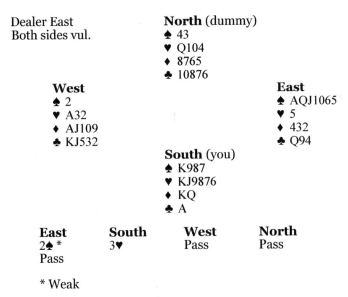

Dealer East
Both sides vul.

**North** (dummy)
♠ 43
♥ Q104
♦ 8765
♣ 10876

**West**
♠ 2
♥ A32
♦ AJ109
♣ KJ532

**East**
♠ AQJ1065
♥ 5
♦ 432
♣ Q94

**South** (you)
♠ K987
♥ KJ9876
♦ KQ
♣ A

| East | South | West | North |
|------|-------|------|-------|
| 2♠ * | 3♥ | Pass | Pass |
| Pass | | | |

\* Weak

Opening lead: ♠2

West leads an obvious singleton and East wins and returns the ♠Q. The contract is made or broken with this play. If you play the ♠K, West ruffs and exits with the ace and a heart leaving you with two more losers, a spade and a diamond. Down one. However, if you duck the ♠K, you will be able to ruff your remaining low spade in dummy. You will also be able to score your ♠K after trumps are drawn. Contract made.

454. When dummy tables with a SOLID side suit plus a side suit singleton, your first consideration should be the side suit, not the singleton suit.

**North** (dummy)
♠ 2
♥ 532
♦ AKQ1098
♣ A98

**South** (you)
♠ J876
♥ AKJ74
♦ J
♣ 543

You wind up in four hearts and West leads a club honor. Instead of worrying about trumping spades, think DIAMONDS, solid diamonds, beautiful diamonds.

Win the ♣A, play the AK of trumps, presumably leaving the queen at large. Next run the diamonds discarding clubs then spades. Eventually the player with ♥Q will trump. No sweat. Dummy's tiny trump is the entry to the remaining diamonds.

What if trump are 4-1? I thought we had decided not to ask questions like that?

455. When the problem is forging reentries to your hand, you can open lines of communication by leading your singleton EARLY in the play.

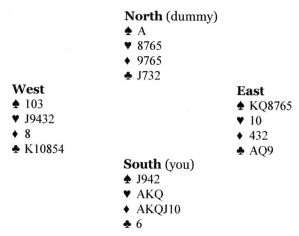

**North** (dummy)
♠ A
♥ 8765
♦ 9765
♣ J732

**West**
♠ 103
♥ J9432
♦ 8
♣ K10854

**East**
♠ KQ8765
♥ 10
♦ 432
♣ AQ9

**South** (you)
♠ J942
♥ AKQ
♦ AKQJ10
♣ 6

In spite of East's one spade opening, thanks to your great bidding, you arrive at a contract of six diamonds. The lead is the ♠10. With a club loser staring you in the face, you must plan to ruff THREE spades on the table.

As it is risky (read suicidal) to enter your hand more than once in hearts, begin by leading a club at trick two. Assume East wins and leads a heart. You win and ruff a spade; back to your hand with a trump to ruff your second spade. Now you have the wherewithal to return to your hand twice with club ruffs. The first to ruff your last spade, the second to draw the remaining trump.

Reentering your hand with a heart BEFORE conceding a club would lead to a very unhappy ending....for you.

# CHAPTER 18

# DECEPTION

Once the dummy comes down and partner is out of the way, you have oh so many opportunities to pull the wool over the opponents' eyes. First, you must recognize the positions. Second, and equally important, is your demeanor. You must make deceptive plays in tempo; if you hesitate you may lose your advantage. Sharp opponents pick up on hesitations.

456.  When a lead marks you with a specific card or cards, play those cards as quickly as possible providing it does not cost you a trick. If you keep the cards you are known to hold, you become an "easy" declarer to play against.

**North** (dummy)
J9732

**West**             **East**
10                 AK654

**South** (you)
Q8

The lead of the ten marks you with the queen. When East wins the first trick, play the queen, the card you are known to hold. For East the location of the eight is now a mystery.

457.

**North** (dummy)
1054

**West**             **East**
Q                 A98732

**South** (you)
KJ6

West leads the queen to East's ace. Drop the king, the card you are known to hold.

458.

**North** (dummy)
K65

**West**             **East**
1098             AQ432

**South** (you)
J7

West leads the 10 of a side suit vs. a suit slam. You play low from dummy and East plays the queen. Drop the jack, the card you are known to hold. East may fear that you have a singleton and shift. This may give you time to discard the seven on another suit. If you play the seven, the jig is up. East knows that the ace will cash.

459. Equally important is to keep any card RHO thinks that LHO may hold from his lead.

**North** (dummy)
9542

**West**　　　　　　　　　　　　　　**East**
J6　　　　　　　　　　　　　　　　　AK87

**South** (you)
Q103

West leads the jack and East plays the king. East knows you have the queen, but does not know who has the ten. If East plays the ace-king, play the queen and the three retaining the ten, the card East thinks West may have.

460. 　　　　　　　　　　　　　**North** (dummy)
965

**West**　　　　　　　　　　　　　　**East**
J2　　　　　　　　　　　　　　　　　A8743

**South** (you)
KQ10

West leads the jack to East's ace and East returns the suit. Play the queen and king, retaining the ten, a card West might have from the lead.

461. Playing cards you are known to hold is a continuing strategy.

**North** (dummy)
76

**West**　　　　　　　　　　　　　　**East**
KJ8432　　　　　　　　　　　　　　Q9

**South** (you)
A105

Versus a suit contract, West leads the four to the queen and ace. Later East leads the nine. Cover with the ten, a card West knows you hold from East's lead of the nine. Now West has to guess who has the five.

462. When LHO leads a likely singleton to partner's ace and you hold three equal honors, play the MIDDLE equal.

**North** (dummy)
8765

**West**　　　　　　　　　　　　　　**East**
2　　　　　　　　　　　　　　　　　A10943

**South** (you)
KQJ

West leads the deuce to East's ace. Play the queen, the MIDDLE card. Perhaps East will play West for KJ2. If you play the jack or the king, East will know that the lead is a singleton. West would not lead the deuce from KQ2 or QJ2.

463. Here is the same idea in a different guise.

                    **North** (dummy)
                    K743
**West**                                    **East**
2                                           A9865
                    **South** (you)
                    QJ10

East has bid the suit and West leads an obvious singleton. When East plays the ace, play the jack, your middle equal. East may misread the lead as low from Q102.

464. Another way to cause confusion and perhaps steal a trick is the "fake finesse".

                    **North** (dummy)
                    K643
**West**                                    **East**
                    **South** (you)
                    QJ

To steal a trick from West, lead the jack. If West ducks and you have a place to dump your queen, mission accomplished.

465. When LHO leads a winning card, signal as if he were your partner. Play low if you do not want the suit continued, high if you do. (This tip assumes that the opponents are playing standard attitude signals, i.e. low-discouraging, high-encouraging).

                    **North** (dummy)
                    975
**West**                                    **East**
AKJ2                                        1064
                    **South** (you)
                    Q83

West leads high and East discourages with the four. If you want this suit continued, play the eight. If you don't, play the three.

466. Withholding a spot card lower than the one that has been led or lower than the one than has been played to your right is sure to wreak havoc in the enemy camp.

**North** (dummy)
AK6

**West**
J853

**East**
1094

**South** (you)
Q72

West leads the three. Most deceptive is to win in dummy playing the seven from your hand. By craftily concealing the deuce East won't know whether West has led from a four or a five card suit and West won't know whether East's four is an encouraging or discouraging signal. You devil, you.

467. In order to conceal weakness in one suit, you may have to feign weakness in another. You may even have to give away a trick to do so. Not to worry! The trick usually comes back with interest. The following examples assume you have a wide open suit that the opponents have NOT led—but you fear they might lead once they get in.

**North** (dummy)
72

**West**
KJ63

**East**
854

**South** (you)
AQ109

West leads low, East plays the eight, and you take the trick with the queen! Not to worry. West will place East with the 1098 and will fall all over himself to return the suit. Once that happens you have three tricks instead of two.

468.

**North** (dummy)
53

**West**
Q9742

**East**
1086

**South** (you)
AKJ

West leads the four and East plays the ten. If you win the KING, West is guaranteed to think East has the jack. If West gets the lead, he is very likely to continue the suit. You get your trick back and West doesn't find the killing shift.

469.

**North** (dummy)
K94

**West**
Q875

**East**
1062

**South** (you)
AJ3

West leads the five, you play low from dummy and East plays the ten. It is perfectly safe to win with the ACE as West is marked with the queen. West will think East has the jack and will be anxious to plug away at this suit. Surprise.

470.

**North** (dummy)
A83

**West**
Q764

**East**
952

**South** (you)
KJ10

West leads the four. You play low from dummy and capture East's nine with the KING. You are giving away NOTHING. West is marked with the queen. West will think East has J109 and when next on lead will waste a tempo continuing the suit. Just what you want.

471.

**North** (dummy)
65

**West**
K10432

**East**
J98

**South** (you)
AQ7

West leads low and East plays the jack. If you win with the ACE, West is sure to play East for the queen. Now take a finesse into WEST. If it loses, West is likely to lead a second low card over to his partner's "known" queen....only you have it!

In order to pull off one of these coups, you must have an equal to the card played to your right and not take the trick with that equal. Instead you must take the trick with a higher card than necessary. Can you get yourself to do this?

472. If you can take a trick with one of two equal cards, use the HIGHER equal.

**North** (dummy)
76

**West**
A10832

**East**
J95

**South** (you)
KQ4

Versus notrump, West leads low and East plays the jack. Win the trick with the KING. West cannot tell who has the queen. If you take the trick with the queen, you give away the show.

473.

**North** (dummy)
97

**West**　　　　　　　　　　　　　　　　**East**
K8532　　　　　　　　　　　　　　　　1064

**South** (you)
AQJ

West leads low and East plays the ten. Win the trick with the queen. Taking the trick with the jack is a nursery school play.

474. When finessing with equals, play the higher equal first.

**North** (dummy)
432

**West**　　　　　　　　　　　　　　　　**East**
K8　　　　　　　　　　　　　　　　　9765

**South** (you)
AQJ10

Whether you lead from dummy or East leads, play the queen. It is too revealing to play a lower honor. If you lead low to the ten and king, East will work out that you remain with the jack and queen. If you lead low to the queen and king, East cannot be sure about the location of the ten and jack.

475. When you want an opponent to cover one of your honors, play your higher or highest equal honor you have.

**North** (dummy)
A2

**West**　　　　　　　　　　　　　　　　**East**
K6　　　　　　　　　　　　　　　　98543

**South** (you)
QJ107

If you want West to play the king, lead the queen.

476. When you do not want an honor covered, play your lower equal.

**North** (dummy)
AK54

**West**　　　　　　　　　　　　　　　　**East**
Q763　　　　　　　　　　　　　　　　982

**South** (you)
J10

Assume this is a side suit with no side entry to dummy. As it stands, the suit is blocked if West plays the queen the first time the suit is played. To reduce this possibility lead the ten. If West plays low, play low from dummy and take three tricks.

477.

**North** (dummy)
2

**West**
A765

**East**
983

**South** (you)
KQJ104

The lead is in your hand. If you want to drive out the ace quickly, play the king. If you want West to duck, play a lower honor.

478. When the king is led and you have small cards in the dummy opposite an AJ combination in your hand, you have several wonderful deceptive options at your disposal.

**North** (dummy)
764

**West**
KQ1093

**East**
82

**South** (you)
AJ5

When West leads the king, play the five. If East plays the eight, West may misread the signal and continue the suit. How bad can that be?

479.

**North** (dummy)
6

**West**
KQ107

**East**
984

**South** (you)
AJ532

West leads the king verses notrump and East discourages with the four. Play the five. With the three and the two missing, West may think the four is an encouraging card and continue the suit.

480. There are even times when it is right to play the jack under the king!

Dealer South
Both vulnerable.

**North** (dummy)
♠ 765
♥ 42
♦ AQJ98
♣ KQJ

**West**
♠ KQ1083
♥ KJ53
♦ 62
♣ 93

**East**
♠ 92
♥ Q976
♦ K54
♣ 10876

**South** (you)
♠ AJ4
♥ A108
♦ 1073
♣ A542

| South | West | North | East |
|-------|------|-------|------|
| 1♣ | 1♠ | 2♦ | Pass |
| 2NT | Pass | 3NT | Pass |
| Pass | Pass | | |

Opening lead: ♠K (Some lead the queen from this holding).

The hand is on ice if West has the ♦K so assume East has it. (Negative assumptions when things look rosy). If you duck the opening lead and East plays the correct deuce, West is sure to shift to a heart. You cannot stand a heart shift. The solution is to play the ♠J at trick one. West will think you have a doubleton and continue the suit. Now you can finesse the diamond safely into East, the opponent who has no more spades. This little move should earn you a little respect.

481. When an opponent leads your concealed suit, a suit in which you have a loser or two, duck the trick. The opening leader will probably think he has struck oil when he has actually struck mud.

**North** (dummy)
32

**West**
QJ98

**East**
76

**South** (you)
AK1054

Versus notrump, West leads the queen. Duck the trick. West is apt to continue.

482.

**North** (dummy)
Q32

**West**　　　　　　　　　　　　　　　**East**
J1097　　　　　　　　　　　　　　　　8

**South** (you)
AK654

Versus notrump West leads the jack. As West is a favorite to have a four card suit, you gain a tempo by ducking. West is likely to continue the suit.

483. Leading towards the closed hand away from honor strength in the dummy frequently produces astonishing results.

**North** (dummy)
AQ65

**West**　　　　　　　　　　　　　　　**East**
982　　　　　　　　　　　　　　　　K1073

**South** (you)
J4

At a suit contract, if you are sure from the bidding that East has the king, cross to the ace and lead low toward your jack. East may think you are planning to trump and duck.

484.

**North** (dummy)
AQ5

**West**　　　　　　　　　　　　　　　**East**
　　　　　　　　　　　　　　　　(Nervous Nellie?)
J1076　　　　　　　　　　　　　　K93

**South** (you)
842

The best way to try for two tricks is to begin by leading the five. If East has the king without the jack, he may pop up with the king. It happens every day.

485.

**North** (dummy)
K765

**West**　　　　　　　　　　　　　　　**East**
1082　　　　　　　　　　　　　　　A943

**South** (you)
QJ

Your best chance to sneak TWO tricks by East is to begin by leading low to the queen. After this holds, reenter dummy and lead low to the jack. If East ducks twice, you have two tricks. What? You don't think East should duck twice? Look at the next diagram.

486.
                        **North** (dummy)
                        K765
        **West**                            **East**
        J82                                 A1043
                        **South** (you)
                        Q9

Play the same, low to the queen, then back to dummy and lead low to your nine. East will have to be looking through the backs of the cards to know whether you started with QJ or Qx.

487.
                        **North** (dummy)
                        Q432
        **West**                            **East**
        J75                                 AK98
                        **South** (you)
                        106

Versus a suit contract, West leads low in a suit East has bid. Dummy plays low and East wins the king, marking the jack with West. Later try leading low towards the ten. East won't know whether you started with 10x or Jx. He may err by playing the ace. Even if East gets it right, think of what you are doing to his nerves.

488.
                        **North** (dummy)
                        AK82
        **West**                            **East**
        J103                                Q765
                        **South** (you)
                        94

Early in a notrump contract you lead the deuce from dummy. East has a tough decision. If East plays the queen, you get three tricks and East gets a lecture.

489.
                        **North** (dummy)
                        AJ104
        **West**                            **East**
        93                                  KQ765
                        **South** (you)
                        82

Versus a suit contract, East bids hearts and West leads the nine. You win with the ace and later lead low towards your eight. East must decide whether you started with 82, 32 or a singleton. In the first case, it is right to rise with an honor, in the other two, it is better to play low.

490. One way to make the opening leader think he has struck gold with his lead is to play an insignificant honor from dummy that you expect will be covered.

**North** (dummy)
A104

**West**
83

**East**
J9762

**South** (you)
KQ5

East has bid the suit and West leads the eight spot (suit or notrump). If you play low from dummy, East will discourage with the deuce and West will know there is no future in the suit. However if you play the ten, East will probably cover. When you take the jack with the king, you may have planted the idea in East's mind that West has the queen. No harm in trying to confuse the issue.

491. Another way to feign weakness is to play two honor cards on the same trick.

**North** (dummy)
KQ

**West**
109876

**East**
543

**South** (you)
AJ2

Versus notrump, take the lead with the ace or underplay the jack. Naive opponents may think you have only two stoppers in the suit. Ha ha.

492. Provided you have the spots, it is far more deceptive to win a trick in dummy than it is to let the lead come around to an equal honor in your hand.

**North** (dummy)
AQ10

**West**
Kxxx

**East**
xxx

**South** (you)
Jxx

If West leads low, play the queen from dummy. If the queen holds, it will be tough for West to know who has the jack. If you win the first trick with the ten, it won't be so tough.

493. With TWO honors in your hand equal to an honor in dummy, play the honor from dummy. It is more deceptive than playing low from dummy.

**North** (dummy)
AQx

**West**
Kxxx

**East**
xxx

**South** (you)
J10x

When West leads low, play the queen from dummy. If the queen wins, West will not know who has the jack. If the queen loses, East may not know you have the jack. If you play low from dummy, bridge players on distant planets will know what you have.

494. Your play at trick one can be affected by their lead conventions.

**North** (dummy)
87

**West**
J10953

**East**
A62

**South** (you)
KQ4

You are playing notrump with a wide open suit. You only need ONE trick in this suit to make your contract. Assume that they play that the lead of a jack denies a higher honor. As you are marked with the KQ, your best shot to encourage a continuation is to play the queen under the ace.

If the lead of the jack can be from the KJ10, play low and hope East continues the suit. WHENEVER A LEAD IS MADE, PARTICULARLY A CONVENTIONAL LEAD, PUT YOURSELF INTO THE HEAD OF THE PARTNER WHO HAS MADE THE LEAD AND PLAY ACCORDINGLY.

495. When conceding inevitable losers, use your HIGHEST equal. Reread this one.

**North** (dummy)
2

**West**
Q1054

**East**
63

**South** (you)
AKJ987

With no dummy entry to take a finesse in your trump suit, you plunk down the ace and the king. When both follow with low cards the ten and the queen remain. As far as losing tricks, it doesn't matter which trump you play at this point—either they break 3-3 or they don't. However for deceptive reasons, play the JACK. If you exit with a low card to the ten, East will know that West has the queen as well. If you exit with the jack to the queen, East will not know (for the moment) who has the ten.

496. In addition, this technique has a way of creating defensive miscues.

**North** (dummy)
543

**West**
K62

**East**
Q7

**South** (you)
AJ1098

This is your trump suit and you have no dummy entries. After you lead the ace continue with the jack. If West is looking for a ruff, he may play high. In addition an inexperienced West player holding Qxx might also take the bait.

497. When the opponents lead a trump and you have a solid trump suit, win the trick with the QUEEN to conceal your strength. The queen is a card you are known to hold because people do not lead a trump from that holding.

**North** (dummy)
765

**West**
832

**East**
109

**South** (you)
AKQJ4

This is your trump suit and West leads low. Win the trick with the queen. East may play West for Axx or Kxx. Whatever you do, do NOT win the trick with the ace. Winning with the ace is like wearing a sign around your neck that says "novice".

498. When LHO leads an honor and RHO is marked with a singleton, try to hold back a spot card lower than the one RHO has played.

**North** (dummy)
KQJ5

**West**
A109764

**East**
3

**South** (you)
82

West shows a six card suit during the bidding and leads the ace. Play the eight. West can no longer be sure who has the deuce. Play the deuce and West will know that the three is a singleton.

499.

**North** (dummy)
Q1075

**West**
AJ9862

**East**
4

**South** (you)
K3

Once again West shows a six card suit and leads the ace. Your best shot to avoid a ruff is to jettison the king under the ace (with no visible hesitation). This may give West the impression that East started with a doubleton.

500. Another way to confuse the issue when RHO plays a known singleton is to withhold TWO higher spot cards.

**North** (dummy)
Q764

**West**  
AKJ108

**East**  
3

**South** (you)
952

West has bid the suit and leads the king (or ace) and you read East's card as a singleton. If West cannot tell from the bidding that East is short, play the deuce. West may think that East started with 953 and not give East the dreaded ruff.

If East is marked with shortness, withhold the deuce giving West the impression that both you and East have a doubleton. This may be enough to discourage a continuation.

501. When LHO leads high from an ace-king combination vs. a suit contract and dummy holds Jxx(x) and you hold the queen, you can quickly discourage a continuation by unloading the queen.

**North** (dummy)
J65

**West**  
AK109

**East**  
862

**South** (you)
Q74

If you cannot afford to lose two tricks in this suit, play the queen at trick one. West will think twice before playing his second honor. If your queen is a singleton, playing a second high honor will establish the jack for a discard.

502. Because a defensive high-low can show either a doubleton or an equal honor, if you have the equal honor, don't play it.

**North** (dummy)
1065

**West**  
AK932

**East**  
84

**South** (you)
QJ7

West leads the ace (ace from ace-king) and East starts a high-low. From West's point of view the eight can either be from shortness or Q84. If West continues with the ace, play the jack and let West work out what the high-low means.

503. When dummy has KJx(x) and you have Qxx, a swindle play looms.

**North** (dummy)
KJ76

**West**
A1043

**East**
82

**South** (the swindler)
QJ95

Assume for one reason or another you wish to take the first two tricks in this suit. Begin by leading low to the KING. Return to your hand and lead low again. West may duck a second time thinking partner has the queen.

504. One way to keep the opponents from attacking your weakest suit is to lead it yourself! Of course, you need the courage of a bulldog to pull this off.

**North** (dummy)
74


**South** (bulldog)
J102

Early in the play of a notrump contract you might try the effect of leading

low to the jack. Strange things are likely to happen after you make a play like this. Don't collapse if your jack wins!

505. Unless you are playing against an expert, assume honest plays are being made against you.

**North** (dummy)
KJ4

**West**
Q10 or Q10x

**East**

**South** (the suspicious one)
A932

You lead low to the jack which wins. Next you play the king and West plays the queen. Who has the ten? If West is not an expert, assume East has it. If West is an expert, he will ALWAYS play the queen from Q10x. (The queen and ten are equals once the jack is played).

Good defenders, like good declarers, play the cards they are known to hold as soon as possible. A taste of your own medicine.

506. One technique to ensure the opponents will continue the suit they have led is to make it just too easy for them to do anything else.

**North** (dummy)
Q54

**West**
J10983

**East**
K762

**South** (you)
A

At a suit contract, West leads the jack. If you want this suit continued, play the queen! Each opponent will assume you have at least one more card in the suit.

507. Do not show off by leading the higher of equals for no reason.

**North** (dummy)
A

**South** (you)
QJ10987

When you cross to dummy lead the seven, not a higher card.

508. If you wish to conceal strength in a suit in which you have all of the honors, at least pretend you are taking a finesse.

**North** (dummy)
AQJ2

**West**
864

**East**
1095

**South** (you)
K73

Assume this is a side suit in either a trump or a notrump contract. When you cross to dummy lead the seven to the queen. East may think you are finessing and West may think that East is holding up. If you cross to the ace, players in Outer Mongolia will know you have the king.

509. Opponents can often be led around like sheep. Whichever suit you seem to be intent on discarding is sure to be the suit they will attack once they get the lead.

**North** (dummy)
♠ AQJ10
♥ 876
♦ Q104
♣ 1054

**South** (you)
♠ 2
♥ AK5
♦ AKJ932
♣ J92

Having missed the 3NT boat, you arrive in five diamonds and get a trump lead. Your best chance is to cross to the ♠A and run the queen of spades, discarding a HEART. If West wins, he will probably shift to a heart rather than a club. Wouldn't you? Once that happens you will have time to discard two clubs on the established spades. If you discard a club on the ♠Q, which suit do you think West will lead upon winning the ♠K?

510. When a normal play is doomed to failure, think swindle.

**North** (dummy)
A4

**West**                                    **East**
K832                                        J109

**South** (you)
Q765

This is a side suit at a suit contract and you cannot afford to lose a trick in the suit. If you lead the queen and West has the king with no serious interior spot cards, he may duck fearing you have a QJ10 or QJ9 combination.

511.                                        **North** (dummy)
                                            AK2

**West**                                    **East**
Q765                                        1093

**South** (you)
J84

If no endplays or squeezes are on the horizon and you have reason to believe the suit is divided 4-3, you might try swinging the jack. West, holding Qxxx, may duck fearing you have J109x.

512.                                        **North** (dummy)
                                            A65

**West**                                    **East**
Q87                                         10942

**South** (you)
KJ3

If you are certain WEST has the queen with length and there is no chance for an endplay or a squeeze, lead the jack. If West has the queen without the ten, West may duck. There are many holdings that you could have where it would be right for West to duck (KJ10, J10x. J10xx, plus others). With your actual holding West will look like the village idiot if he doesn't cover.

Ironically these swindle plays are more apt to work against a good player than against an average player. Most average players cover every honor in sight.

513. At notrump when LHO leads top of nothing smack into your strongest suit, your job is to make RHO think that LHO has led fourth best. It isn't always easy.

**North** (dummy)
93

**West**             **East**
7654             J82

**South** (you)
AKQ10

West leads the seven, East plays the jack and you must take this trick with a card that will deceive East into thinking that West has strength in the suit. To do this look at your cards and project a holding where the seven is a normal fourth best lead. For instance, if you take the trick with the ace, East will know that you are falsecarding. If the ace were a true card, West would have started with KQ107 and would not lead the seven. If you win with the queen, East may also have cause for pause. If this is a true card, West started with AK107 and might have led high. But if you take the trick with the KING, East may believe that West has led fourth best from an AQ107 combination and return the suit upon gaining the lead.

514. If you wish to induce the opponents to lead a trump, lead dummy's short suit—even if you have nothing to trump in that suit. If one opponent thinks you have something to trump, you may see the desired trump on the table. You're so tricky.

515. In order to steal two tricks with KQJxx in dummy facing xx(x) in your hand, force the player with the ace to play to the second round of the suit first. In that way, the player with the ace may not be able to read partner's count signal.

**North** (dummy)
KQJ98

**West**             **East**
764             A52

**South** (you)
103

Assume East has the ace. Lead the TEN to the jack which East ducks. Next lead the king from dummy. East cannot be sure whether West's four is from

764 or 43. If it is the latter, East must duck again. This play is particularly effective when dummy has no side entry.

Note: players who use upside-down count signals will have no trouble with this one. West signals with the seven originally, showing an odd number of cards, and East will know to win the second round of the suit.

516. Faking a finesse with a solid type suit is often a good way to fool your LHO.

**North** (dummy)
Q6

**West**　　　　　　　　　　　　　　　　**East**
A7　　　　　　　　　　　　　　　　　9532

**South** (you)
KJ1084

Say you begin by leading low to the queen which holds. On the second round of the suit lead low from dummy and play the ten from your hand. West may think that you started with K109xx and that partner remains with

Jx. If your intention is to fool East, play low to the queen and then low to the jack. East may think that West started with A10x.

It might be amusing to end the section with one of the most deceptive hands ever played. The deal is from a tournament played in France many years ago.

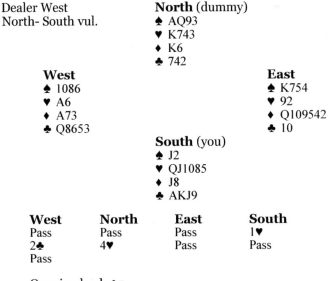

Dealer West
North- South vul.

**North** (dummy)
♠ AQ93
♥ K743
♦ K6
♣ 742

**West**
♠ 1086
♥ A6
♦ A73
♣ Q8653

**East**
♠ K754
♥ 92
♦ Q109542
♣ 10

**South** (you)
♠ J2
♥ QJ1085
♦ J8
♣ AKJ9

| West | North | East | South |
|------|-------|------|-------|
| Pass | Pass | Pass | 1♥ |
| 2♣ | 4♥ | Pass | Pass |
| Pass | | | |

Opening lead: ♣5

It was apparent to South (the heroine) that East had a singleton club. Furthermore South realized that if she won the trick with the jack, West would also know that East started with a singleton and would hasten to give East a ruff.

South began her deception by winning the first trick with the ace. Who could blame West for thinking that East had the jack?

South continued with the jack of trump in order to induce West to duck and forestall a second club play. West won the second heart and innocently led a club over to partner's supposed jack. Surprise South had the jack! South had now retrieved the club trick she had given away earlier to avoid the ruff.

South was just getting warmed up. As the bidding had marked West with the ace of diamonds, South tried another "fake finesse" by leading the jack. When West ducked, South won the trick with the king.

It was now apparent that East had the K♠ as West was a passed hand and had already turned up with 10 HCP. Well, if two fake finesses had already worked, why not try to fake a ruff? South cashed the ace of spades and led a low spade toward the jack. East ducked. South still wasn't through. With two trump entries remaining in dummy, South crossed to a trump and swung the queen of spades. This time West covered and South ruffed splattering the ten. Dummy was reentered with a club ruff and the losing diamond discarded on the ♠9. Making six! South had made a deceptive play in all four suits.

# CHAPTER 19

# THE SIMPLE SQUEEZE

Most players fear the word "squeeze" figuring that executing one is beyond them. Actually, with a few basics understood, squeezes are not that frightening at all. The few examples that follow should give you the general idea.

The first step is to be able to distinguish a threat suit from a non-threat suit

517. A threat suit is ANY suit from which an extra trick can be realized if the defenders can be forced to discard enough cards in that suit.

**North** (dummy)
A65

**West**          **East**
Q1084          J932

**South** (you)
K7

This is a threat suit. If East and West each discard twice from this suit, dummy's third card is a winner. You may ask, why would they each discard twice from this suit? Because they may each be forced to guard another suit.

518. A non-threat suit is a suit in which you cannot make an extra trick regardless of the number of discards the opponents make in the suit.

**North** (dummy)
KQ4

**South** (you)
A32

This is a non-threat suit. No matter how many cards the opponents throw away in this suit, you cannot score more than three tricks.

519. When you are playing a contract that has at least two threat suits, you may have a squeeze!

520. When the same opponent is the sole guard of two or more threat suits, he is a prime candidate for a squeeze.

521. Most squeezes are easiest to execute when you have all the tricks but one.

When you arrive at such a position (frequent), the trick is to play each and every one of your non-threat winners before your threat suit winners. Reread that. In the case of a suit contract it usually means playing each and every winning trump. (Some players become emotionally involved with their trump suit and will not part with the last one. These players may play a lifetime without operating a squeeze)!

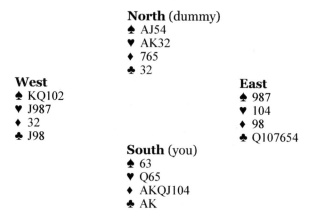

**North** (dummy)
♠ AJ54
♥ AK32
♦ 765
♣ 32

**West**
♠ KQ102
♥ J987
♦ 32
♣ J98

**East**
♠ 987
♥ 104
♦ 98
♣ Q107654

**South** (you)
♠ 63
♥ Q65
♦ AKQJ104
♣ AK

You arrive at seven diamonds and the opening lead is the ♠K. You have 12 tricks (all but one) with two threat suits, hearts and spades. The ingredients are there. Play all of your non-threat winners (diamonds and clubs) first.

The squeeze takes place on the LAST non-threat winner. This is what it will look like when you play your last diamond (or your last club).

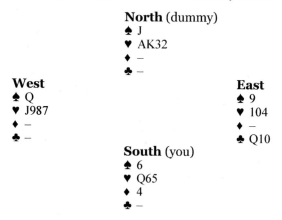

**North** (dummy)
♠ J
♥ AK32
♦ –
♣ –

**West**
♠ Q
♥ J987
♦ –
♣ –

**East**
♠ 9
♥ 104
♦ –
♣ Q10

**South** (you)
♠ 6
♥ Q65
♦ 4
♣ –

When you play the ♦4, West must discard. West cannot release the ♠Q because that will make the jack high. Perforce West must give up a heart. You discard the now worthless ♠J and take the last four heart tricks.

522. When both threat cards are in the SAME hand (in the previous example North has both threats, the J♠ and the long heart), you can only squeeze the player that plays BEFORE North. In this case, West. If the East-West hands were interchanged there would be no squeeze. East would be discarding after North. East discards the same suit North discards on the last non-threat suit winner. Dummy is squeezed before East.

523. When your two threat suits are in opposite hands (happiness), you can squeeze either player who happens to be guarding both suits.

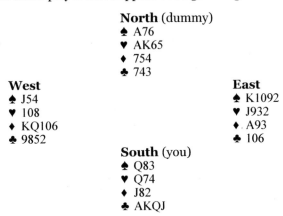

North (dummy)
♠ A76
♥ AK65
♦ 754
♣ 743

West
♠ J54
♥ 108
♦ KQ106
♣ 9852

East
♠ K1092
♥ J932
♦ A93
♣ 106

South (you)
♠ Q83
♥ Q74
♦ J82
♣ AKQJ

You land in 3NT and the defense starts with four rounds of diamonds. East discarding an encouraging spade. You, in the meantime, discard a club from dummy and a spade from your hand.

At trick five West shifts to a low spade. You rise with the ace and assess your chances. You have eight top tricks with threats in two suits. The ♠Q is a threat in your hand and the fourth heart is a threat in dummy. Your threats are divided! You can squeeze either player who happens to have four or more hearts along with the ♠K. In this case East is your victim. All you have to do is cash your non-threat suit winners first. Play four rounds of clubs, discarding two spades from dummy. East can discard a spade on the third club but the fourth club squeezes East into submission.

524. In order to operate a squeeze, at least one of the threat suits must have an entry. In the last hand hearts was the entry suit as the spade switch removed the entry in that suit.

525. Some THREAT suits have entries to only one hand (AKx in dummy facing xx in your hand), a "one-way" entry threat suit. Some threat suits have entries to both hands (Kx facing Axx), a "two-way" entry threat suit. First the bad news.

When you only have a one-way entry threat suit, you must arrange to cash your LAST non-threat suit WINNER ending in the hand OPPOSITE the entry. Cheer up. This tip is almost over.

The good news. If you have a threat suit that has an entry in both hands (Kx facing Axx), you can end up in either hand after cashing your non-threat suit winners.

**North** (dummy)
♠ AKQ4
♥ 32
♦ AKQJ
♣ KQ4

**South** (you)
♠ 32
♥ AJ4
♦ 9876
♣ AJ108

You arrive at a contract of 7NT and West leads the ♥K. You have 12 top tricks with threats in two suits. You have a heart threat (the jack) in your hand and a spade threat in dummy. Only one suit has an entry...spades. It is a one-way entry threat suit. The entry is in the NORTH hand. Your plan should be to run off your non-threat suit winners ending in YOUR hand. Translation: cash your diamonds before your clubs. Had your spades been Qx facing AKxx, a threat suit with entries to both hands, you could have cashed the clubs and diamonds in any order.

526. Because most squeezes operate best when you have all the tricks but one, it may be necessary to concede inevitable losers to arrive at this position.

527. In order to determine how many tricks you must concede before going into your squeeze mode, subtract the number of sure tricks you have from twelve. Say you are playing a contract of 3NT and you have eight sure tricks with a couple of threat suits. By subtracting 8 from 12 you discover that you must concede four before going into your act. All these early ducking or concession plays go under the highfalutin' moniker of "rectifying the count". It sounds scary, but you can do it.

528. When you have THREE threat suits and must concede a trick in order to rectify the count, concede it in the threat suit that both opponents are sure to control. In other words, the least threatening threat suit.

**North** (dummy)
♠ 42
♥ K65
♦ AQ43
♣ AK54

**West**
♠ KQJ95
♥ 87
♦ 98
♣ 10876

**East**
♠ 10876
♥ J1092
♦ J1076
♣ 3

**South** (you)
♠ A3
♥ AQ43
♦ K52
♣ QJ93

Disdaining the superior contract of six clubs, you wind up in 6NT. West makes the obvious lead of the ♠K.

Count tricks. You have eleven top tricks with "serious" threats in two suits; hearts and diamonds. Spades is also a threat suit but not as serious.

When you subtract your sure tricks (11) from the magic number 12, you determine that you must duck a trick in order to rectify the count. Duck the opening lead and concede a trick in your least serious threat suit.

Assume a spade is continued to your ace. Your play is to run your non-threat suit winners first. Clubs is your only non-threat suit so play four rounds of clubs.

Take a gander at the East hand. East must make three discards. East has two easy spade discards but the last discard is painful. Whichever red suit East releases gives you a trick and your contract.

## THE BOTTOM LINE —SIMPLE SQUEEZE INGREDIENTS

529. At least two threat suits; one of which must have an entry to it.

530. All the tricks but one. Duck tricks, if necessary, to arrive at this position.

531. Avoid at all costs ducking a trick in a threat suit and turning it into a non-threat suit. You would only dream of doing this if you had three or four threat suits. Very rare.

532. Take your tricks in your non-threat suits before your tricks in your threat suits.

533. When one threat suit has a one-way entry and the other does not, plan to cash your non-threat suit winners ending in the hand opposite that entry.

534. When one threat suit has built-in entries to both hands, you can cash your non-threat suit winners in any order.

535. If you are playing the hand in a trump contract and you arrive at a position where you have all of the tricks but one, your trump suit takes on the role of non-threat suit. Translation: play every trump before playing the threat suits.

536. You are only allowed to scream for joy after you pull off your first squeeze. After that, you must act as if it were a matter of course.

# CHAPTER 20

# TIPS FOR TOURNAMENT PLAYERS

The play of the hand at tournament bridge is at times so far removed from the play at rubber bridge or team of four scoring as to be unrecognizable.

In rubber or team scoring the objective is to make your contract— overtricks be damned! At tournament bridge, overtricks are so important that you routinely risk your contract to make one lousy overtrick. No one wins matchpoint events by taking the same number of tricks as Mr. and Mrs. Jones.

Having said that, do not think that you risk your contract on every hand for an overtrick or two. There are mitigating circumstances.

537. Before you begin the play ask yourself two questions:

   (1) What contract do I expect the other pairs with our cards to be playing?

   (2) How do I rate the contract I am in? Is it great, favorable, routine or hopeless? To a large extent your line of play is based upon the answers to these two questions.

538. If you are playing in a great contract, a contract that you do not expect the field to reach, play safe. If a safety play is possible, make it. Just bringing home a "great contract" means a top or near top score. A board won in the bidding should not be given back in the play.

539. Play doubled contracts the same way you play great contracts— as safely as possible. You can only get one top on a board.

**North** (dummy)
♠ A93
♥ K5432
♦ Q10
♣ 762

**South** (you)
♠ KJ542
♥ —
♦ AKJ92
♣ QJ10

West doubles your final contract of four spades (does he know who you are?) and leads the king, ace and a third club, East following up the line.

Without the double, you would try for an overtrick by leading a spade to the ace and a spade to the jack. With the double, your only concern is making the contract. A safety play in spades is called for. Lead the king and then low to the nine if West follows low. If West shows out on the second spade, win the ace and lead low to the jack. You have just guarded against a 4-1 trump split in either hand in order to ensure your doubled contract.

540. Make no safety plays or overly cautious plays in normal contracts. Go for the throat.

**North** (dummy)
♠ Q43
♥ KJ10
♦ 97
♣ AKJ43

**South** (you)
♠ KJ2
♥ Q87653
♦ A5
♣ Q2

You wind up in four hearts and West leads the ♦Q. If you begin by knocking out the ♥A, you make your contract easily. You lose one heart, one diamond and one spade. However if you attack clubs before hearts, you make an overtrick if clubs are 3-3. If clubs break 4-2 you break even.

You get rid of your diamond loser (the good news) but somebody ruffs your third club (the bad news). The really bad news is when clubs are 5-1. Your second club gets ruffed and down you go in an ice cold contract. No matter. To play hearts before clubs is no way to win a tournament.

541. The idea of risking a normal contract for an overtrick or two (if there is a reasonable chance of success) cannot be emphasized strongly enough.

**North** (dummy)
♠ 3
♥ K9
♦ AQ109872
♣ Q83

**South** (you)
♠ AKQ42
♥ A8
♦ 65
♣ KJ104

You may recognize this hand. It is in the section on notrump play. In that section it was suggested that with a heart lead you can ensure NINE tricks by driving out the ♣A.

Playing duplicate bridge attack diamonds, not clubs. You have more than a 50% chance of bringing in either six or seven diamond tricks before the opponents can establish their hearts. Lead a diamond to the queen at trick two. If this loses and a heart comes back, plunk down the ♦A. If the jack doesn't drop, there will always be another tournament.

542. If you want to play for a swing in a normal contract, play a key suit abnormally. As long as you are not bucking the odds too greatly, you have a chance of scoring a top...or a bottom.

**North** (dummy)
♠ A54
♥ K54
♦ QJ3
♣ K983

**South** (you)
♠ KJ8763
♥ 32
♦ K105
♣ A2

After partner opens one club, you wind up in four spades which you judge to be a normal contract. West leads the ♥Q and eventually you ruff the third round of hearts.

Everything is riding on the trump suit. The field will play the ace-king. If you wish to buck the field, play the ace and then low to the jack. You will either get a near top, or a near bottom. You will not get an average!

543. If you are playing in an inferior contract, judge what score the other pairs in your direction will probably be making. Take almost any risk imaginable to tie or beat that score.

**North** (dummy)
♠ K32
♥ K432
♦ A43
♣ A52

**West**
♠ 64
♥ 1098
♦ QJ109
♣ KJ84

**East**
♠ J985
♥ 76
♦ K76
♣ Q973

**South** (you)
♠ AQ107
♥ AQJ5
♦ 852
♣ 106

After an awful bidding misunderstanding (partner's fault), you wind up in four spades, and West leads the ♦Q. The field will surely be in four hearts. PROJECT THE PLAY IN FOUR HEARTS TO DETERMINE WHAT THE OTHER PAIRS ARE GOING TO SCORE. If hearts are 3-2 and the ♠J comes down allowing for a diamond discard, the players in hearts will take 11 tricks. Your maximum in spades is 10 tricks. The only way you can tie this board is to assume that spades are NOT breaking and East has four to the jack. If that is the case, the pairs in hearts will only take 10 tricks and you can at least tie those pairs by taking a third-round spade finesse.

Doing all this analyzing is not much fun, but it is what you have to do when your partner puts you in a lousy contract.

544. Do not risk an extra undertrick with a "far out" play which, if it works, will allow you to make your contract. Let the others go for the "far out" plays.

**North** (dummy)
♠ 76
♥ A87
♦ KJ1076
♣ A65

**South** (you)
♠ A5
♥ KJ102
♦ Q92
♣ KJ43

You wind up in 3NT and the lead is the ♠2. As spades appear to be 5-4, you can settle for down one by driving out the ♦A. However you do have a chance to make this hand. If East has both the ♥Q and precisely ♣Qxx, you can bring home nine tricks. However if either finesse loses, you will go down two. It is asking a bit much of the bridge Gods to not only put two queens in the right place but have another suit split 3-3 as well. At rubber bridge or team scoring, play to make. At matchpoints, settle for down one.

545. One number to avoid when playing a competitive part score contract is -200 (the kiss of death). Assuming the cards are somewhat equally divided, a score of -200 invariably gives the opponents a top or near-top score.

546. When you take a save vs. an UNMAKEABLE slam, you may still be able to salvage a few match points. Your new goal is to go down in your "sacrifice" fewer points than the opponents would have made had they stopped in game.

Dealer East
North- South vul.

**North** (dummy)
♠ K7654
♥ —
♦ A10543
♣ 654

**South** (you)
♠ AQJ1032
♥ 7
♦ KJ62
♣ 93

| West | North | East | South |
|------|-------|------|-------|
| 1♥ | 1♠ | 4♥ | 4♠ |
| 5♥ | 5♠ | 6♥ | 6♠ |
| Dbl. | Pass | Pass | Pass |

Opening lead: ♣K

West continues with the ♣Q and a club to East's ace which you ruff. When you play the ace of spades, all follow.

Unless someone has a diamond void, you have taken a phantom sacrifice. Assuming neither opponent is void, you still have to consider what is going to happen at the other tables. Perhaps East-West will buy the hand for five hearts. Assuming 5H can be made, East-West will score +450 at some tables. Therefore, lousy sacrifice or not, you can still salvage some match points if you can hold your loss to down ONE doubled.

Unless the opponents are completely mad, diamonds are 3-1. Now the question is: which opponent is more likely to have two singletons? Given the bidding, it sounds like West. Play the ♦A and lead low to the jack.

547. When your side takes a sacrifice against a game contract, the assumption is that the opponents can make game. Plan the play on the assumption that they can make their contract. If they can't, you are not slated for a good match point score.

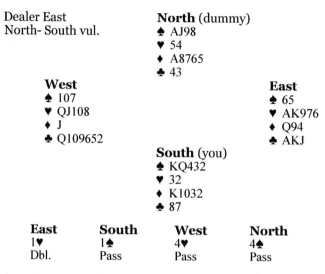

Dealer East
North- South vul.

North (dummy)
♠ AJ98
♥ 54
♦ A8765
♣ 43

West
♠ 107
♥ QJ108
♦ J
♣ Q109652

East
♠ 65
♥ AK976
♦ Q94
♣ AKJ

South (you)
♠ KQ432
♥ 32
♦ K1032
♣ 87

| East | South | West | North |
|------|-------|------|-------|
| 1♥   | 1♠    | 4♥   | 4♠    |
| Dbl. | Pass  | Pass | Pass  |

Opening lead: ♥Q

East overtakes with the king, cashes the ♣AK, the ♥A, and exits with a trump. When you play a second trump, both follow.

The only way this is going to be a good sacrifice is if diamonds are 3-1. If diamonds are 2-2, you are destined for a bad score. Presumably some of the North-South pairs (including those that did not overcall one spade with your hand) will go plus defending four hearts. Your only chance to salvage the board is to not only hope that diamonds are 3-1, but also that West has a singleton honor (the only 3-1 distribution that allows you to pick up the suit without losing a trick). Lead a diamond to the ace willing an honor to fall from West. When it does, lead a diamond to the ten. Your masterful play in diamonds holds your losses to down one, beating all the wimpy North-South pairs that sold out to 4♥.

548. A typical matchpoint play problem arises when you wind up in three notrump having missed a 4-4 major suit fit. As the field figures to be in the major, determine how many tricks can be made in the major and set out to take at least that number, risks or no risks.

164

**North** (dummy)
♠ 52
♥ AJ82
♦ K10874
♣ Q10

**South** (you)
♠ Q76
♥ KQ109
♦ A3
♣ AK74

Having "miraculously" avoided your 4-4 heart fit, you wind up in 3NT. West leads the ♠J and your first break comes when East plays the king, ace and a third spade to your queen.

The good news is that you now have 10 top tricks. The bad news is that if you take those 10 tricks you will wind up with a bottom! Every Tom, Dick and Harry will be taking 11 tricks in hearts. Your only chance is to go for 11 tricks. Lead a low club to the ten. If it works you have a top; if it loses, you have the same bottom you would have had settling for 10 tricks.

549. The opening lead, to a large extent, determines the play. Opening leads come in three packages: 1) normal—what you expect will be led at the other tables; 2) favorable— giving you a present; 3) unfavorable—something that could only happen to you. The killing lead!

When a normal opening lead gives you a reasonable chance for an overtrick (at the risk of your contract), it is usually right to go for it.

Dealer South
Neither side vul.

**North** (dummy)
♠ A7
♥ J86
♦ 103
♣ QJ9874

**South** (you)
♠ Q
♥ Q3
♦ AK76
♣ AK10532

| South | West | North | East |
|-------|------|-------|------|
| 1♣    | 2♠*  | 3♣    | 4♠   |
| 5♣    | Pass | Pass  | Pass |

*Weak

Opening lead: ♠6

On the reasonable assumption that West has the ♠K, duck the lead to your queen gambling for the overtrick. Not only will you beat all the other pairs who played the ace from dummy with the same lead, but you will also beat those pairs who received a heart lead. In addition, your score of +420 will defeat those pairs who played 3NT from the North seat and received a spade lead. Their score of +400 won't beat yours either.

550. When blessed with a favorable lead, maintain your plus position by not taking any unnecessary risks.

**North** (dummy)
- ♠ 86
- ♥ AJ4
- ♦ AK863
- ♣ 1076

**South** (you)
- ♠ A7
- ♥ K732
- ♦ 42
- ♣ KQJ82

Having bid every suit in sight except spades, you arrive in 3NT. Incredibly, West leads the ♦J. This opening lead gives you an easy nine tricks with the possibility of even more, if you eventually take the heart finesse after driving out the ♣A and getting a belated spade shift.

However there is no need to go for overtricks. At the other tables, a spade will surely be led. With a spade lead, the other declarers will all go minus. Having been once blessed, don't get greedy. You don't have to.

551. When cursed with a lead that is unlikely to be made at the other tables, you must recover lost ground by doing something unusual.

Dealer West
Neither side vul.

**North** (dummy)
- ♠ AK
- ♥ 653
- ♦ J1084
- ♣ 10965

**South** (you)
- ♠ 2
- ♥ Q4
- ♦ AQ96
- ♣ AKQJ87

| West | North | East | South |
|------|-------|------|-------|
| 2♠ | Pass | 4♠ | 5♣ |
| Pass | Pass | Pass | |

Opening lead: ♥2

166

East wins the first two heart tricks with the king and ace and continues with the jack which you ruff high, West following.

Before falling all over yourself to take the diamond finesse, consider what has happened to you. West has made an opening lead out of the blue that has already cost you one trick. At the other tables a spade is likely to be led allowing those declarers to discard a heart.

In order to get that trick back you must go against the field in another suit. The only suit around is diamonds. Do not take the finesse. Play West for a singleton king! It is your only chance to recover the board.

Think about it. If you take the diamond finesse and it works you will make your contract. Congratulations. The only problem is that the other declarers will be making six. Same scenario if the diamond finesse loses. You will go down one.... they will make five.

552. If you are playing a tough partscore contract on a hand that either side could declare, play to go plus—any plus will do. When the high cards are rather equally divided, some pairs sitting your direction are sure to go minus. To have a plus score on a competitive hand is to be sitting pretty.

553. Avoid the temptation of making hold-up plays if things can work out so well that you may not have to lose those tricks.

**North** (dummy)
♠ 65
♥ AQJ1054
♦ A3
♣ 876

**South** (you)
♠ A73
♥ 92
♦ K842
♣ AKQ5

After you open 1NT, you wind up in 3NT. West leads the ♠K. Do not hold up! You might make 13 tricks if both hearts and clubs come in. Ducking even once excludes that chance.

Furthermore if you hold up twice, you can no longer beat the pairs in hearts because they will not have to lose two spade tricks. Say hearts are trumps and a spade is led. If the heart finesse loses, declarer still takes 11 tricks beating the ten tricks maximum you will take if you duck two spades.

If the heart finesse works, the declarers in hearts are going to make 12 or 13 tricks while you, playing notrump,have already ducked two spades! Help! Win the opening lead and run the nine of hearts.

554. Because luck plays such a serious role in most matchpoint events, one must learn to roll with the punches. If the opponents do a couple of crazy things

that work out, the tendency is to go even crazier to get the board(s) back, a losing strategy.

Sooner or later the gifts will start coming your way. You don't want to have such a poor game that when they finally arrive (and they will) you cannot take advantage of it.

555. Make the opponents pay for their errors. If a defensive error gives you a chance for a top, go for it rather than settle for an above average score.

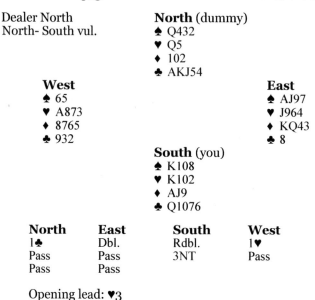

Dealer North
North- South vul.

**North** (dummy)
♠ Q432
♥ Q5
♦ 102
♣ AKJ54

**West**
♠ 65
♥ A873
♦ 8765
♣ 932

**East**
♠ AJ97
♥ J964
♦ KQ43
♣ 8

**South** (you)
♠ K108
♥ K102
♦ AJ9
♣ Q1076

| North | East | South | West |
|-------|------|-------|------|
| 1♣ | Dbl. | Rdbl. | 1♥ |
| Pass | Pass | 3NT | Pass |
| Pass | Pass | | |

Opening lead: ♥3

You play low from dummy and capture East's jack. At trick two you lead a spade to the queen and ace, East continuing a heart to West's ace. West returns a third heart to your ten.

Before discarding from dummy, it might be wise to take stock. You and your partner have 25 HCP leaving the opponents with 15. As West has already shown up with 4 HCP, it is reasonable to assume that East has ALL the missing honor cards for his takeout double.

Your play is to discard a diamond from dummy, cross to dummy with a club and finesse the ♠10. When that holds, cash the ♠K and run the clubs. The last club squeezes East between diamonds and spades. Making five should be worth a bundle of matchpoints. Had East shifted to a high diamond upon winning the ace of spades or if West had shifted to a low diamond upon winning the ace of hearts, the squeeze would have been broken up for lack of communication.

Compare this to tip #14. In that tip you had a SURE top by playing safe for your contract. In this tip you are taking a small risk to improve from a slightly above average score to a likely tie for top score.

556. When you see an opponent "steaming" because either you or your partner has done something unusual that has worked or because his partner has done something that hasn't, brace yourself. The steamer is going to try to get it ALL back. Keep your cool, hope your partner does the same and wait for another good result.

557. No matter what the dummy looks like, no matter how impossible the contract appears, no matter how you feel about your partner at the moment, remember your goal:

TAKE ALL YOUR TRICKS!

# BONUS TIPS

- The quickest road to disaster is to stop thinking about the contract you are in — thinking instead about the contract you wish you were in. Before you know it, you will be playing the hand as if you were in that other contract.

- When RHO bids a suit and LHO leads a trump, LHO has: (1) a balanced hand with honors in each suit; (2) Axx in partner's suit and fears you may have the king; (3) a hearing disorder.

- A player who leads a short suit seldom has the queen of trumps. Play RHO for the queen.

- The more bids the opponents make, the easier it is to count the hand. With a little bit of luck you will know each player's distribution once the dummy comes down.

- It is usually not necessary to count both hands. Once a player either turns up with a long suit or has shown a long suit in the bidding, work with that hand. It makes life easier.

- Watch the opponent's signals. In case of ambiguity, a trusty high-low or low-high may clarify the position.

- If you can take the same number of tricks at notrump as you can at your suit contract, convert to notrump at once. Do not fall into the trap of trumping a loser that can be discarded later.

- Before drawing trump, decide where you want to end up. Don't surprise yourself.

- When you have a weak suit that you wish to conceal and must give up the lead in a side suit, do not draw trump. You may give an opponent a chance to make a revealing discard.

# ABOUT THE AUTHOR

*EDWIN B. KANTAR*
*Member of the Bridge Hall of Fame*
*Teacher, Writer, National & World Champion*

Eddie Kantar, a transplanted Californian (originally from Minneapolis, MN), is one of the best known bridge writers in the world. He has written over 30 bridge books. He is also a regular contributor to the ACBL Bulletin, Bridge World, Bridge Today, and OK. Bridge.

Eddie, a two-time World Champion, is highly regarded as a player, and he still competes regularly on the National level. He is known as one of bridge's great ambassadors. He learned to play bridge at 11 and by the time he was 17 he was teaching professionally —and still is!

As a player Eddie gained stature by winning Two World Championships, a dozen National Championships, and countless Regional and Sectional titles. His North American titles include the Spingold and Vanderbilt Knockout Teams, the Reisinger Board-a-Match Teams and the Grand National Teams. Eddie is a Grand Master in the World Bridge Federation rankings and an ACBL Grand Life Master with more than 10,000 master points.

Presently, Eddie lectures on bridge cruises, and takes groups twice a year for one week all inclusive bridge holidays to beautiful hotels on the Mexican Riviera. He also teaches occasionally in the Los Angeles area as well as lecturing several times a year in various resort areas in the U.S. and Canada.

Today, Eddie is best known as a writer and many of his books are considered classics. Many of his books have been translated into other languages, including "Bridge for Dummies" which has been translated into two languages thus far. He has won the American Bridge Teacher's Association award for "Best Book of the Year" 4 times. When not writing about bridge, Eddie can be found at Venice Beach playing paddle tennis, an offshoot of tennis, a sport in which he has also garnered several trophies. Since many of the paddle tennis players are also bridge players, often a bridge game is formed there as well!

By the way, Eddie is the only person ever to have played in a World Bridge Championship and a World Table Tennis Championship. He had more success in the Bridge World Championship. Eddie was inducted into the Bridge Hall of Fame in 1996, the same year he was inducted into the Minnesota State Table Tennis Hall of Fame

# OTHER BOOKS BY EDWIN B. KANTAR

**EDDIE KANTAR TEACHES MODERN BRIDGE DEFENSE**

Awarded the American Bridge Teachers' Association "1999 Best Intermediate Bridge Book of the Year" Also available in CD-ROM EDITION

**EDDIE KANTAR TEACHES ADVANCED BRIDGE DEFENSE**

Awarded the American Bridge Teachers' Association "1999 Best Advanced Bridge Book of the Year" Also available in CD-ROM EDITION

**EDDIE KANTAR TEACHES TOPICS IN DECLARER PLAY**

An intermediate level book on the play of the hand dealing with Entries, Long Suit Establishment, Finessing, Strip and End Plays and the dreaded Counting. Rave Reviews .

CD- ROM: Eddie Kantar Teaches Topics in Declarer Play. This interactive edition is an educational and fun software product that presents the same material as the book in interactive mode. Test yourself with many quizzes that follow.

**CLASSIC KANTAR**

A collection of Eddie's best humorous bridge stories.

**BRIDGE FOR DUMMIES**

Awarded the American Bridge Teachers' Association "1997 Best Beginning Bridge Book of the Year"

**ROMAN KEY CARD BLACKWOOD**

Slam bidding for the 21st century (advanced).

**IMPROVE YOUR BIDDING SKILLS**

Standard bidding methods in quiz form.

**BRIDGE CONVENTIONS**

Popular conventions fully explained.

**A TREASURY OF BRIDGE TIPS**

540 bidding tips to improve your partner's game.

TEST YOUR PLAY, Volume 1

100 play problems, intermediate to advanced.

TEST YOUR PLAY, Volume 2

100 play problems, intermediate level.

CD-ROM Play and Defend with Eddie Kantar. Hands from Test Your Play Vol. 2. This interactive edition presents 100 neat intermediate play problems. Each hand is followed by commentaries and tips. Guaranteed to help your play of the hand.

INTRODUCTION TO DECLARER'S PLAY

A basic primer on the play of the hand.

INTRODUCTION TO DEFENDER'S PLAY

Beginning defensive concepts, including signaling and opening leads.

KANTAR FOR THE DEFENSE, Volume 1

100 Defensive problems - Intermediate/advanced level.

KANTAR FOR THE DEFENSE, Volume 2

100 more challenging intermediate/advanced defensive problems.

DEFENSIVE TIPS FOR BAD CARD HOLDERS

If you continually pick up lousy hands, this book is for you.

A NEW APPROACH TO PLAY AND DEFENSE

Hands to play and then similar hands to defend.

A NEW APPROACH TO PLAY AND DEFENSE, Vol. 2

More hands to play and then defend. CD-ROM Play and Defend with Eddie Kantar

GAMESMAN BRIDGE

The trials and tribulations of trying to teach someone who thinks he knows how to play.

52 FACTS OF BRIDGE LIFE

For all of these books and more, visit www.kantarbridge.com.